Trackers Plus

Tracking children's progress through the Early Years Foundation Stage

by
Colin Gallow

Attach photograph here

A QEd Publication

Published in 2009

© Colin Gallow

Development matters statements are taken from *The Early Years Foundation Stage* (DCFS, 2008).

ISBN 978 1 898873 64 8

All rights reserved. This book is sold subject to the condition that it shall not, by way of trade or otherwise, be lent, hired out or otherwise circulated without the publisher's prior consent in any form other than that in which it is published.

With the exception of pages 28, 50, 63, 82, 95, 111 and 113-120 no part of this publication may be reproduced, stored in a retrieval system, or transmitted in any form or by any means, electronic, mechanical, photocopying, recording or otherwise, without the prior written permission of the publisher.

British Library Cataloguing
A catalogue record for this book is available from the British Library.

Published by QEd Publications, 39 Weeping Cross, Stafford ST17 0DG
Tel: 01785 620364
Fax: 01785 607797
Website: www.qed.uk.com
Email: orders@qed.uk.com

Acknowledgements
Hannah Mortimer for her clear thinking and practical advice.
Deborah Falshaw and staff at the Horn End Nurseries for their suggestions.
Ann Ross for her valuable contributions.
The numerous childminders, early years advisers and nursery staff for their feedback.

Printed by Gutenberg Press Ltd, Malta.

Contents

	Page
Introduction	4
Guidance for parents and carers	4
Guidance for early years staff and childminders	4
All about me	8
Area of Learning – Personal, Social and Emotional Development	9
Dispositions and Attitudes	10 - 12
Self-confidence and Self-esteem	13 - 15
Making Relationships	16 - 18
Behaviour and Self-control	19 - 21
Self-care	22 - 24
Sense of Community	25 - 27
Area of Learning – Communication, Language and Literacy	29
Language for Communication	30 - 33
Language for Thinking	34 - 36
Linking Sounds and Letters	37 - 39
Reading	40 - 43
Writing	44 - 46
Handwriting	47 - 49
Area of Learning – Problem Solving, Reasoning and Numeracy	51
Numbers as Labels and for Counting	52 - 54
Calculating	55 - 57
Shape, Space and Measures	58 - 62
Area of Learning – Knowledge and Understanding of the World	64
Exploration and Investigation	65 - 67
Designing and Making	68 - 70
ICT	71 - 72
Time	73 - 75
Place	76 - 78
Communities	79 - 81
Area of Learning – Physical Development	83
Movement and Space	84 - 87
Health and Bodily Awareness	88 - 90
Using Equipment and Materials	91 - 94
Area of Learning – Creative Development	96
Being Creative – Responding to Experiences, Expressing and Communicating Ideas	97 - 100
Exploring Media and Materials	101 - 104
Creating Music and Dance	105 - 107
Developing Imagination and Imaginative Play	108 - 110
Appendix	
Final Summative Assessment Comments	112
Assessment Scales	113 - 120

Introduction

Guidance for parents and carers

Whatever setting your child is in, whether in a nursery or with a registered childminder, the overall aim will be to help your child:

- develop as a unique individual;
- form positive relationships with others;
- feel ready to develop, to play and to learn.

From September 2008 all early years providers had to meet certain standards set out in the Early Years Foundation Stage (EYFS). One of the requirements is that members of staff use ongoing observations to monitor how your child is developing and learning and use these to plan their play and learning. There are many different ways in which observations can be made. One method of keeping track of all these observations is to use *Trackers Plus*.

The Trackers are divided into the Areas of Learning that fit in with the EYFS framework. They relate to children aged 0 to 5 and show all the many steps that young children pass through before they go to school and into the year in which they start.

The EYFS divides children's experiences into six Areas of Learning. Within these, there are also certain Early Learning Goals (highlighted in the text) which most children will be expected to reach before the end of the year in which they reach their fifth birthday.

Trackers Plus is also useful for sharing valuable information with parents or carers, enabling you to keep in touch with your child's progress and allowing a much closer partnership with the setting. There is a box for **Evidence and Progression** notes after each Development matter stage, and a general observation and planning form at the end of each Area of Learning for you to add any comments you wish to make.

It is important to remember that each child is unique and no two will follow exactly the same pathway of development. Remember too that these early steps in playing and learning are very important if your child is going to be able to make good progress later on. Play is how young children learn and we should not rush them into more formal teaching and learning until they are ready. So please do not be concerned if there are gaps in your child's record. It might be that staff members have not yet had the opportunity to observe that area recently or that your child is busy making progress in other ways. Children do things at very different ages and stages.

Guidance for early years staff and childminders

The Early Years Foundation Stage

All early years practitioners are expected to plan and provide play opportunities which foster **a unique child**, **positive relationships**, **enabling environments** and **learning and development**. To help them achieve this, there are EYFS resources such as a CD-ROM, poster and Principle into Practice cards. There is also EYFS Practice Guidance which contains non-statutory guidance, additional advice and a set of Learning and development grids. These describe the steps that many children go through as they collect experiences and gather learning opportunities on their path towards the **Early Learning Goals**.

Keeping track

Many practitioners have found it helpful to have an individual progress record for each child in their care. This enables them to track progress, know at a glance how each child is playing and learning, and serve as the basis for forward planning and talking with parents and carers. *Trackers Plus* serves this purpose and should be used alongside (rather than instead of) the ongoing observational assessment which informs your planning for each child's continuing development.

Trackers Plus provides a method of tracking, or following, a child's development through the EYFS. They are not a curriculum in themselves; the framework you should be following is fully described in the Early Years Foundation Stage Statutory Framework and the Early Years Foundation Stage Practice Guidance.

Who the Trackers are for

These progress trackers will be useful for early years educators working in all kinds of early years settings: childminders, nursery classes, foundation classes, pre-schools, playgroups, private nurseries, day nurseries and creches. It will also be helpful for individuals training on NVQ or early childhood education courses and of interest to parents and carers of children who are interested in tracking and supporting their children's development through the EYFS.

The six Areas of Learning

These Trackers have been designed to be simple and usable, yet to link into the Government's *Early Years Foundation Stage* (Department for Children, Schools and Families, 2008). The guidance focuses on how children learn and what adults can do to encourage that learning. It identifies six Areas of early learning:

- Personal, Social and Emotional Development.
- Communication, Language and Literacy.
- Problem Solving, Reasoning and Numeracy.
- Knowledge and Understanding of the World.
- Physical Development.
- Creative Development.

Early Learning Goals

Within each Area of Learning, there are Early Learning Goals which most children will be expected to reach by the end of their Reception year. The Trackers show all the areas of development within each particular Area of Learning, and weave in some of the skills-based stages through the use of examples in the right hand column.

The statements of developmental stages, skills, understanding or competence that appear under the heading **Examples** are there to help clarify some of the **Development matters** statements, or simply to provide a prompt.

How to use Trackers Plus

Use one progress Tracker booklet for each child. Observe the child during your daily play and care activities and keep a note of your ongoing observations in the **Evidence and progression notes** spaces provided. If you feel that the child has reached that particular stage most of the time (we all have good days and bad days), you can record this in the Trackers, recording the date of your observation and the relevant information in the evidence column. Revisit the Trackers at regular intervals. You will then find that you are gradually able to observe and record more and more steps as the child develops and gathers experiences.

Example

Choose a system of observation and recording to suit your setting and keep it simple [there is lots of useful information about observation in *The Observation and Assessment of Children in the Early Years* (Mortimer, 2008)].

Below is an example of one section in *Trackers Plus* with notes added in the **Evidence and progression** box. Each note that is added is dated with the initials of the person writing the note (this is important because it is an ongoing record).

You might wish to record that a child was unwell for a while in order to explain why there was a setback in their confidence. You might add a comment that a child went into hospital for grommets on a certain date and that might explain why speech and understanding suddenly improved. Or you could add qualifying comments such as 'only if a familiar adult is present'.

Make sure that you have actual evidence for each of the items you record. Work on your *actual* observations rather than on hearsay. This is simply because you need to know which items still need encouragement or teaching and which are well established as part of the child's repertoire.

Area of Learning	Personal, Social and Emotional Development
Focus	Dispositions and Attitudes

	Development matters	**Dates achieved**	**Examples**
30 – 50 months	• Seek and delight in new experiences.	06/04/08	• Chooses between activities.
	• Have a positive approach to activities and events.		• Delights in own successes.
			• Knows likes and dislikes.
	• Show confidence in linking up with others for support and guidance.		• Shows a sense of pride in own achievement.
			• Plays happily in a large group.
	• Show increasing independence in selecting and carrying out activities.	01/05/08	• Begins to settle for 5 to 10 minutes on an activity.

Evidence and progression notes

[20/12/07 M.J] Sam tried new activity (block building) when prompted.
To do: Talk to Sam early in session to help him plan ahead.

[06/04/08 M.J] Often tries things he's not tried before (e.g. drawing program on the PC today).
[07/04/08 S.G] Tends to prefer being on his own (reads, or playing with Lego). But often watches other children playing together.
To do: Activity 4.3 in Music Makers to help Sam join in with the group.

[01/05/08 M.J] When doing the 'Visiting Day' activity, I tracked Sam's progress – he was involved in the Home Corner, the Early Writing, added to the Display, and the Outdoor activity with bears (showing great independence and choice).

Planning the observations and providing evidence

Some settings find it easiest to delegate responsibility for the tracking to different members of staff. For example, each child should be assigned to one key person who could be responsible for tracking the development of a small group of children. Other settings might ascribe a certain Area of Learning to a particular member of staff who would also have the responsibility for planning and developing opportunities and activities in that area for that term.

Plan certain activities or opportunities which are going to allow you to observe a particular aspect of all the children's development that session, for example sand play with small and large buckets to encourage the understanding of size. Always aim for a balance between adult-led and child-initiated activity.

Make all observations in as natural a way as possible so that the children are not aware of a different situation or the fact that you are observing them.

At the back of the book you will find the EYFS profile – assessment scales (taken from the guidance). You may find this useful as a summary chart of progress.

Remember that *Trackers Plus* form just one aspect of your ongoing observation and planning. You can collect a variety of observational evidence through sources such as children's work, photographs and parent/carer input. These will help you to track significant achievements in each child's learning and allow you to plan for their developmental needs. Find regular opportunities to share progress with parents and carers. Compare notes and share successes.

Meeting individual needs

As part of your regular observation, you may notice that a particular child is developing rather patchily or following a different pathway. Perhaps there is one or more aspect of their development that is not progressing as fast as the others. This provides you with useful information for planning new learning opportunities for that child. Because the progress Trackers make you aware of the possible 'next steps' that each child passes through, you can play alongside the child to teach and encourage an appropriate next step. Remember that each child is unique and follows his or her own pathway of development.

Sometimes you might be aware that a child has SEN because their development is significantly different from what you would normally expect for that age. You will also need to refer to *The Special Educational Needs Code of Practice* (DfES, 2001) for further guidance on meeting their needs or refer to *The SEN Code of Practice in Early Years Settings* published by QEd Publications. You will also find *Playladders* (Mortimer, 2008) a useful tool for observing and supporting children with special needs in your setting.

It is important that you *communicate* with parents or carers regarding the progress Trackers. Parents may be alarmed if they see that a large number of statements have not been 'achieved' and may fear that their child is not progressing. These Trackers should not be seen as a definitive guide to a child's progress, they simply represent one further way of observing, recording and tracking progress. Sometimes parents may need reassuring that it is quite normal for children's development to progress at very different rates.

References

DfES (2001) *The Special Educational Needs Code of Practice*. Nottingham: DfES Publications.
DCFS (2008) *The Early Years Foundation Stage*. Nottingham: DfES Publications.
Mortimer, H. (2002) *The SEN Code of Practice in Early Years Settings*. Stafford: QEd Publications.
Mortimer, H. (2008) *Playladders*. Stafford: QEd Publications.
Mortimer, H. (2008) *The Observation and Assessment of Children in the Early Years*. Stafford: QEd Publications.

All about me

Name: _____ Date of Birth : _____

Age: _____ Date: _____

This is my family (including pets):

I am good at:

My friends are:

My favourite activity is:	**My favourite toy is:**

I like it when:

I get upset when:

I need help with:

© QEd Publications

Area of Learning

Personal, Social and Emotional Development

Aspects of Personal, Social and Emotional Development

- Dispositions and Attitudes – how children become interested, excited and motivated about their learning.

- Self-confidence and Self-esteem – about children having a sense of their own value and understanding the need for sensitivity to significant events in their own and other people's lives.

- Making Relationships – about the importance of children forming good relationships with others and working alongside others.

- Behaviour and Self-control – how children develop a growing understanding of what is right and wrong and why, together with learning about the impact of their words and actions on themselves and others.

- Self-care – how children gain a sense of self-respect and concern for their own personal hygiene and care and how they develop independence.

- Sense of Community – how children understand and respect their own needs, views, cultures and beliefs and those of other people.

from *The Early Years Foundation Stage* (DCFS, 2008)

Area of Learning	Personal, Social and Emotional Development
Focus	Dispositions and Attitudes

	Development matters	**Dates achieved**	**Examples**
Birth – 11 months	• Develop an awareness and understanding of themselves. • Learn that they have influence on and are influenced by others. • Learn that experiences can be shared.		• Enjoys looking at faces. • Coos and gurgles when happy. • Plays with own fists and feet. • Plays peek-a-boo games. • Puts arms up to be lifted. • Smiles at own reflection.

Evidence and progression notes

	Development matters	**Dates achieved**	**Examples**
8 – 20 months	• Become aware of themselves as separate from others. • Discover more about what they like and dislike. • Have a strong exploratory impulse. • Explore the environment with interest.		• Watches other children when held close. • Turns when you call their name. • Shows when dislikes something. • Interested in new people and toys. • Repeats play sequences (e.g. putting in/emptying out). • Willing to explore new activities with support.

Evidence and progression notes

© QEd Publications

Area of Learning	Personal, Social and Emotional Development
Focus	Dispositions and Attitudes

	Development matters	**Dates achieved**	**Examples**
16 – 26 months	• Learn that they are special through the responses of adults to individual differences and similarities. • Develop a curiosity about things and processes. • Take pleasure in learning new skills.		• Knows who to go to for help. • Knows where to find toys. • Follow the routines of the session easily. • Willing to try new experiences. • Explores the playroom.

Evidence and progression notes

	Development matters	**Dates achieved**	**Examples**
22 – 36 months	• Show their particular characteristics, preferences and interests. • Begin to develop self-confidence and a belief in themselves.		• Copes with changes in routine. • Calls out to others to attract their attention. • Enjoys being with other children. • Repeats an action to get a response. • Is keen and interested in the activities.

Evidence and progression notes

© QEd Publications

Area of Learning	Personal, Social and Emotional Development
Focus	Dispositions and Attitudes

	Development matters	**Dates achieved**	**Examples**
30 – 50 months	• Seek and delight in new experiences. • Have a positive approach to activities and events. • Show confidence in linking up with others for support and guidance. • Show increasing independence in selecting and carrying out activities.		• Chooses between activities. • Delights in own successes. • Knows likes and dislikes. • Shows a sense of pride in own achievement. • Plays happily in a large group. • Begins to settle for 5 to 10 minutes on an activity.

Evidence and progression notes

	Development matters	**Dates achieved**	**Examples**
40 – 60 months	• Display high levels of involvement in activities. • Persist for extended periods of time at an activity of their choosing. • **Continue to be interested, excited and motivated to learn.** • **Be confident to try new activities, initiate ideas and speak in a familiar group.** • **Maintain attention, concentrate, and sit quietly when appropriate.**		• Finds own equipment. • Becomes very involved when playing favourite activity. • Takes risks and explores within the setting. • Concentrates on an activity for over 20 minutes. • Actively involves others in play. • Shows another child ways of playing with a toy.

Evidence and progression notes

© QEd Publications

Area of Learning	Personal, Social and Emotional Development
Focus	Self-confidence and Self-esteem

	Development matters	**Dates achieved**	**Examples**
Birth – 11 months	• Seek to be looked at and approved of. • Find comfort in touch and in the human face. • Thrive when their emotional needs are met. • Gain physical, psychological and emotional comfort from 'snuggling in'.		• Gurgles and coos when given attention. • Is comforted by close body contact • Snuggles in when held.

Evidence and progression notes

	Development matters	**Dates achieved**	**Examples**
8 – 20 months	• Feel safe and secure within healthy relationships with key people. • Sustain healthy emotional attachments through familiar, trusting, safe and secure relationships. • Express their feelings within warm, mutual, affirmative relationships.		• Separates from parent/carer with confidence. • Enjoys having approval. • Looks happy and settled even when an adult is not nearby. • Shares a laugh and a chuckle. • Enjoys the company of other children.

Evidence and progression notes

© QEd Publications

Area of Learning	Personal, Social and Emotional Development
Focus	Self-confidence and Self-esteem

	Development matters	Dates achieved	Examples
16 – 26 months	• Make choices that involve challenge, when adults ensure their safety. • Explore from the security of a close relationship with a caring and responsive adult. • Develop confidence in own abilities.		• Able to make choices in play. • Can cope with new people, children, activities if a familiar person is nearby. • Can tell you which setting they go to, and talk about what they do there.

Evidence and progression notes

	Development matters	Dates achieved	Examples
22 – 36 months	• Begin to be assertive and self-assured when others have realistic expectations of their competence. • Begin to recognise danger and know who to turn to for help. • Feel pride in their own achievements.		• Able to set challenges in their play. • Asserts self if someone takes a toy he/she is playing with. • Avoids dangers when playing. • Seeks help when it is needed. • Draws others' attention to something they are proud of.

Evidence and progression notes

Area of Learning	Personal, Social and Emotional Development
Focus	Self-confidence and Self-esteem

	Development matters	Dates achieved	Examples
30 – 50 months	• Show increasing confidence in new situations. • Talk freely about their home and community. • Take pleasure in gaining more complex skills. • Have a sense of personal identity.		• Continues to feel content when not the centre of attention. • Can handle changes in regular routine. • Talks about self and own experiences. • Willing and happy to play with children who are new to the setting. • Happy to talk and share ideas in a large group.

Evidence and progression notes

	Development matters	Dates achieved	Examples
40 – 60 months	• Express needs and feelings in appropriate ways. • Have an awareness and pride in self as having own identity and abilities. • **Respond to significant experiences, showing a range of feelings when appropriate.** • **Have a developing awareness of their own needs, views and feelings, and be sensitive to the needs, views and feelings of others.** • **Have a developing respect for their own cultures and beliefs and those of other people.**		• Lets you know when feeling angry/anxious/sad in appropriate ways. • Feels positively about him/herself. • Lets you know what his/her needs are, in appropriate ways. • Adapts behaviour to different occasions. • Has an awareness and pride in self and recognises they are unique with abilities. • Shows care and concern for others.

Evidence and progression notes

© QEd Publications

Area of Learning	Personal, Social and Emotional Development
Focus	Making Relationships

	Development matters	Dates achieved	Examples
Birth – 11 months	• Enjoy the company of others and are sociable from birth. • Depend on close attachments with a special person within their setting. • Learn by interacting with others.		• Recognises main carer. • Enjoys being sociable. • Likes to have a familiar adult nearby. • Calls out for attention, comfort and play.

Evidence and progression notes

	Development matters	Dates achieved	Examples
8 – 20 months	• Seek to gain attention in a variety of ways, drawing others into social interaction. • Use their developing physical skills to make social contact. • Build relationships with special people.		• Pulls or tugs at adult to gain attention. • Starts to play with other children. • Moves close to others sometimes as he/she plays.

Evidence and progression notes

© QEd Publications

Area of Learning	Personal, Social and Emotional Development
Focus	Making Relationships

	Development matters	Dates achieved	Examples
16 – 26 months	• Look to others for responses which confirm, contribute to, or challenge their understanding of themselves. • Can be caring towards each other.		• Seeks out others to share experiences. • Greets people appropriately. • Makes attachments to other children. • Can share toys with adult support.

Evidence and progression notes

	Development matters	Dates achieved	Examples
22 – 36 months	• Learn social skills, and enjoy being with and talking to adults and other children. • Seek out others to share experiences. • Respond to the feelings and wishes of others.		• Enjoys playing with an adult. • Happy to play alongside others. • Can tell you who their friends are. • Can share a toy with another child. • Recognises when others are happy/sad/angry.

Evidence and progression notes

© QEd Publications

Area of Learning	Personal, Social and Emotional Development
Focus	Making Relationships

	Development matters	**Dates achieved**	**Examples**
30 – 50 months	• Feel safe and secure, and show a sense of trust. • Form friendships with other children. • Demonstrate flexibility and adapt their behaviour to different events, social situations and changes in routine.		• Initiates interactions with others. • Will join in a group in the home corner. • Talks about who their friends are. • Adapts how he/she behaves to fit in with others. • Enjoys playing cooperatively with other children.

Evidence and progression notes

	Development matters	**Dates achieved**	**Examples**
40 – 60 months	• Value and contribute to own well-being and self-control. • **Form good relationships with adults and peers.** • **Work as part of a group or class, taking turns and sharing fairly, understanding that there needs to be agreed values and codes of behaviour for groups of people, including adults and children, to work together harmoniously.**		• Shows care and concern for others. • Works in a group. • Understands the need for behaviour rules. • Understands what is right/wrong and why. • Considers consequences for others of what they do (e.g. 'If I snatch this toy my friend will be upset').

Evidence and progression notes

Area of Learning	Personal, Social and Emotional Development
Focus	Behaviour and Self-control

	Development matters	Dates achieved	Examples
Birth – 11 months	• Are usually soothed by warm and consistent responses from familiar adults. • Begin to adapt to caregiving routines.		• Likes to have a familiar adult nearby. • Looks towards a familiar carer when upset. • Lets adult know when cross/upset/happy by behaving differently.

Evidence and progression notes

	Development matters	Dates achieved	Examples
8 – 20 months	• Respond to a small number of boundaries, with encouragement and support.		• Follows simple routines and simple boundaries. • Accepts having nappy changed. • Stops pulling your hair when asked.

Evidence and progression notes

© QEd Publications

Area of Learning	Personal, Social and Emotional Development
Focus	Behaviour and Self-control

	Development matters	Dates achieved	Examples
16 – 26 months	• Begin to learn that some things are theirs, some things are shared, and some things belong to other people.		• Knows that some things are theirs and some things need to be shared. • Accepts 'no' without too much fuss. • Understands 'yes' and 'no'. • Begins to share toys (sometimes with adult support).

Evidence and progression notes

	Development matters	Dates achieved	Examples
22 – 36 months	• Are aware that some actions can hurt or harm others.		• Aware that some things they do, such as scratching and pushing, can hurt others. • Shows care and concern when others are upset.

Evidence and progression notes

© QEd Publications

Area of Learning	Personal, Social and Emotional Development
Focus	Behaviour and Self-control

	Development matters	Dates achieved	Examples
30 – 50 months	• Begin to accept the needs of others, with support. • Show care and concern for others, for living things and the environment.		• Shows care and concern for living creatures. • Behaves in a way that makes others feel happy/settled. • Aware that plants and trees need caring for. • Knows when some wrong has been done to them and tells adult. • Tells you when they see others treated hurtfully.

Evidence and progression notes

	Development matters	Dates achieved	Examples
40 – 60 months	• Show confidence and the ability to stand up for own rights. • Have an awareness of the boundaries set, and of behavioural expectations in the setting. • **Understand what is right, what is wrong, and why.** • **Consider the consequences of their words and actions for themselves and others.**		• Understands and accepts the need for rules in games. • Understands and respects others' needs (e.g. why I should be quiet or gentle). • Considers the consequences of their actions (e.g. 'If I snatch this toy my friend will be upset).

Evidence and progression notes

© QEd Publications

Area of Learning	Personal, Social and Emotional Development
Focus	Self-care

	Development matters	Dates achieved	Examples
Birth – 11 months	• Anticipate food routines with interest. • Express discomfort, hunger or thirst.		• Looks interested at food times. • Tugs at wet or dirty nappy. • Raises arms to bottle.

Evidence and progression notes

	Development matters	Dates achieved	Examples
8 – 20 months	• Begin to indicate own needs, for example, by pointing. • May like to use a comfort object.		• Points to the foods or drinks they want. • Pulls off socks. • Holds arms or legs up when being dressed.

Evidence and progression notes

Area of Learning	Personal, Social and Emotional Development
Focus	Self-care

	Development matters	**Dates achieved**	**Examples**
16 – 26 months	• Show a desire to help with dress and hygiene routines. • Communicate preferences.		• Wants to try some things 'all by myself'. • Uses the potty successfully with reminders. • Tries to wash own hands. • Indicates a choice by pointing. • Indicates when toilet needed with accidents.

Evidence and progression notes

	Development matters	**Dates achieved**	**Examples**
22 – 36 months	• Seek to do things for themselves, knowing that an adult is close by, ready to support and help if needed. • Become more aware that choices have consequences. • Take pleasure in personal hygiene including toileting.		• Makes a choice and sticks by it. • Joins in simple routines (e.g. moving the chairs). • Can indicate choice by using yes/no. • Has successes in the potty. • Puts on hat or shoes. • Helps to wash and dry own hands.

Evidence and progression notes

© QEd Publications

Area of Learning	Personal, Social and Emotional Development
Focus	Self-care

	Development matters	**Dates achieved**	**Examples**
30 – 50 months	• Show willingness to tackle problems and enjoy self-chosen challenges. • Demonstrate a sense of pride in own achievement. • Take initiatives and manage developmentally appropriate tasks.		• When playing, tries different things (tools/objects) to make 'it' work. • Asks for help and guidance with confidence. • Fetches coat/apron at the right time.

Evidence and progression notes

	Development matters	**Dates achieved**	**Examples**
40 – 60 months	• Operate independently within the environment and show confidence in linking up with others for support and guidance. • Appreciate the need for hygiene. • **Dress and undress independently and manage their own personal hygiene.** • Select and use activities and resources independently.		• Begins to set up, and clear away activities when finished. • Washes hands before eating and after using the toilet. • Chooses the resources needed for an activity and tidies up afterwards.

Evidence and progression notes

© QEd Publications

Area of Learning	Personal, Social and Emotional Development
Focus	Sense of Community

	Development matters	Dates achieved	Examples
Birth – 11 months	• Respond to differences in their environment, for example, showing excitement or interest. • Learn that special people are a source of sustenance, comfort and support.		• Shows different behaviours and reactions in different situations. • Pleased to be greeted when arriving. • Makes sounds when an adult speaks to them.

Evidence and progression notes

	Development matters	Dates achieved	Examples
8 – 20 months	• Learn that their voice and actions have effects on others.		• Cries differently due to different discomforts. • Shouts to attract attention. • Indicates wish for a drink when thirsty.

Evidence and progression notes

© QEd Publications

Area of Learning	Personal, Social and Emotional Development
Focus	Sense of Community

	Development matters	**Dates achieved**	**Examples**
16 – 26 months	• Learn that they have similarities and differences that connect them to, and distinguish them from, others.		• Knows that they are like others in certain ways (type of clothes, hair colour and so on). • Knows that there are some things special to them (e.g. their physical appearance).

Evidence and progression notes

	Development matters	**Dates achieved**	**Examples**
22 – 36 months	• Show a strong sense of self as a member of different communities, such as their family or setting. • Show affection and concern for special people.		• Can tell you the names of four or five other children. • Talks easily to familiar adults. • Talks easily to other children. • Talks about who their friends are.

Evidence and progression notes

© QEd Publications

Area of Learning	Personal, Social and Emotional Development
Focus	Sense of Community

	Development matters	**Dates achieved**	**Examples**
30 – 50 months	• Make connections between different parts of their life experience.		• Can tell you where they live. • Talks about home when they are in the setting. • Brings things from home to share or show.

Evidence and progression notes

	Development matters	**Dates achieved**	**Examples**
40 – 60 months	• Have an awareness of, and an interest in, cultural and religious differences. • Have a positive self-image, and show that they are comfortable with themselves. • Enjoy joining in with family customs and routines. • **Understand that people have different needs, views, cultures and beliefs, that need to be treated with respect.** • **Understand that they can expect others to treat their needs, views, cultures and beliefs with respect.**		• Interested in the ways different people live. • Happy to talk about where they belong – 'my family, my group, my community'. • Shows confidence and able to stand up for their rights. • Shows respect for others.

Evidence and progression notes

© QEd Publications

General Observation and Planning Form

Activity	Comments	Member of staff/ parent/carer	Date

© QEd Publications

Area of Learning

Communication, Language and Literacy

Aspects of Communication, Language and Literacy

- Language for Communication – how children become communicators. Learning to listen and speak emerges out of non-verbal communication which includes facial expression, eye contact, and hand gesture. These skills develop as children interact with others, listen to and use language, extend their vocabulary and experience stories, songs, poems and rhymes.

- Language for Thinking – how children learn to use language to imagine and recreate roles and experiences . . . how they use talk to clarify their thinking and ideas or refer to events they have observed or are curious about.

- Linking Sounds and Letters – how children develop the ability to distinguish between sounds and become familiar with rhyme, rhythm and alliteration. They develop understanding of the correspondence between spoken and written sounds and learn to link sounds and letters and used their knowledge to read and write simple words by sounding out and blending.

- Reading – about children understanding and enjoying stories, books and rhymes, recognising that print carries meaning, both fiction and fact, and reading a range of familiar words and simple sentences.

- Writing – how children build an understanding of the relationship between the spoken and written word and how through making marks, drawing and personal writing children ascribe meaning to text and attempt to write for various purposes.

- Handwriting – the ways in which children's random marks, lines and drawings develop and form the basis of recognisable letters.

from The Early Years Foundation Stage (DCFS, 2008)

Area of Learning	Communication, Language and Literacy
Focus	Language for Communication

	Development matters	Dates achieved	Examples
Birth – 11 months	• Communicate in a variety of ways including crying, gurgling, babbling and squealing. • Make sounds with their voices in social interaction.		• Cries when distressed. • Uses early sounds and noises as signals for you to give attention. • Gurgles or squeals when cuddled or tickled.

Evidence and progression notes

	Development matters	Dates achieved	Examples
8 – 20 months	• Take pleasure in making and listening to a wide variety of sounds. • Create personal words as they begin to develop language.		• Babbles in long strings (e.g. 'ma - ma - ma'). • Uses one or two words consistently as labels (e.g. mama and dada). • Makes up some sounds/words to mean things.

Evidence and progression notes

© QEd Publications

Area of Learning	Communication, Language and Literacy
Focus	Language for Communication

	Development matters	Dates achieved	Examples
16 – 26 months	• Use single-word and two-word utterances to convey simple and more complex messages. • Understand simple sentences.		• Eager to use words to 'tell you' things. • Uses single words to tell you what they want (e.g. 'di' for 'drink'). • Uses two-word utterances (e.g. 'mama car').

Evidence and progression notes

	Development matters	Dates achieved	Examples
22 – 36 months	• Learn new words very rapidly and are able to use them in communicating about matters which interest them.		• Asks for toys using words. • Uses two or more recognisable words together. • Responds to simple instructions. • Can use 10 clear words.

Evidence and progression notes

Area of Learning	Communication, Language and Literacy
Focus	Language for Communication

	Development matters	Dates achieved	Examples
30 – 50 months	• Use simple statements and questions often linked to gestures. • Use intonation, rhythm and phrasing to make their meaning clear to others. • Join in with repeated refrains and anticipate key events and phrases in rhymes and stories. • Listen to stories with increasing attention and recall. • Describe main story settings, events and principal characters. • Listen to others in one-to-one or small groups when conversation interests them. • Respond to simple instructions. • Question why things happen and give explanations. • Use vocabulary focused on objects and people that are of particular importance to them. • Begin to experiment with language describing possession. • Build up vocabulary that reflects the breadth of their experiences. • Begin to use more complex sentences. • Use a widening range of words to express or elaborate on ideas.		• Asks simple questions. • Makes simple statements/comments during play. • Listens to others in a small group. • Sometime starts a conversation. • Gives simple explanations. • Uses describing words (e.g. 'big') and possession words (e.g. 'mine'). • Uses familiar phrases (e.g. 'once upon a time ...'). • Follows simple direction words such as in/on/under. • Uses intonation, rhythm and phrasing when talking to you. • Speaks in more complex sentences (e.g. using other possessive words like his, her, your). • Asks simple 'where' questions.

Evidence and progression notes

Area of Learning	Communication, Language and Literacy
Focus	Language for Communication

	Development matters	**Dates achieved**	**Examples**
40 – 60 months	- Have confidence to speak to others about their own wants and interests. - Use talk to gain attention and sometimes use action rather than talk to demonstrate or explain to others. - Initiate conversation, attend to and take account of what others say. - Extend vocabulary, especially by grouping and naming. - Use vocabulary and forms of speech that are increasingly influenced by their experience of books. - Link statements and stick to a main theme or intention. - Consistently develop a simple story, explanation or line of questioning. - Use language for an increasing range of purposes. - Use simple grammatical structures. - **Interact with others, negotiating plans and activities and taking turns in conversation.** - **Enjoy listening to and using spoken and written language, and readily turn to it in their play and learning.** - **Sustain attentive listening, responding to what they have heard with relevant comments, questions or actions.** - **Listen with enjoyment, and respond to stories, songs and other music, rhymes and poems and make up their own stories, songs, rhymes and poems.** - **Extend their vocabulary, exploring the meanings and sounds of new words.** - **Speak clearly and audibly with confidence and control and show awareness of the listener.**		- Talks with confidence to visitors. - Uses 50 words to talk about things of interest. - Uses other children's names when speaking to them. - Listens and responds to group instructions. - Sticks more or less to the topic of conversation. - Retells a simple story. - Uses language for increasing range of purposes (ask for information, to describe, remember and to explain). - Turn-takes in a conversation. - Is aware of the listener's point of view (e.g. pauses to make sure you are listening). - Uses words, tones and phrases from familiar books. - Makes up stories, songs and rhymes. - Answers questions about a story. - Uses simple grammatical structures (e.g. plurals, negatives, questions). - Uses greetings, 'please' and 'thank you' regularly.
Evidence and progression notes			

Area of Learning	Communication, Language and Literacy
Focus	Language for Thinking

	Development matters	**Dates achieved**	**Examples**
Birth – 11 months	• Are intrigued by novelty and events and actions around them.		• Makes sounds when adult speaks to them. • Turns eyes towards person talking. • Uses actions and sounds together to tell you what they need (e.g. when hungry).

Evidence and progression notes

	Development matters	**Dates achieved**	**Examples**
8 – 20 months	• Understand simple meanings conveyed in speech. • Respond to the different things said to them when in a familiar context with a special person.		• Follows familiar instructions (e.g. clap hands). • Points to some body parts when named. • Responds to familiar requests in familiar contexts (e.g. responds to simple directions).

Evidence and progression notes

© QEd Publications

Area of Learning	Communication, Language and Literacy
Focus	Language for Thinking

	Development matters	Dates achieved	Examples
16 – 26 months	• Are able to respond to simple requests and grasp meaning from context.		• Responds to simple requests in familiar contexts (e.g. points to a named picture). • Gives you a named object. • Anticipates what happens next in a familiar rhyme.

Evidence and progression notes

	Development matters	Dates achieved	Examples
22 – 36 months	• Use action, sometimes with limited talk, that is largely concerned with the 'here and now'. • Use language as a powerful means of widening contacts, sharing feelings, experiences and thoughts.		• Uses words to say what they are doing when playing. • Asks 'what?' and 'why?' questions. • Uses simple language and behaviour to tell others how they feel.

Evidence and progression notes

© QEd Publications

Area of Learning	Communication, Language and Literacy
Focus	Language for Thinking

	Development matters	Dates achieved	Examples
30 – 50 months	• Talk activities through, reflecting on and modifying what they are doing. • Use talk to give new meanings to objects and actions, treating them as symbols for other things. • Use talk to connect ideas, explain what is happening and anticipate what might happen next. • Use talk, actions and objects to recall and relive past experiences.		• Uses language with other children in order to sustain play. • Talks through what they are doing while playing. • Manages to control impulses some of the time by thinking before acting. • Talks through something that is going to happen to them in the near future.

Evidence and progression notes

	Development matters	Dates achieved	Examples
40 – 60 months	• Begin to use talk instead of action to rehearse, reorder and reflect on past experience, linking significant events from own experience and from stories, paying attention to how events lead into one another. • Begin to make patterns in their experience through linking cause and effect, sequencing, ordering and grouping. • Begin to use talk to pretend imaginary situations. • **Use language to imagine and recreate roles and experiences.** • **Use talk to organise, sequence and clarify thinking, ideas, feelings and events.**		• Talks about a simple sequence (e.g. 'First we had tea, then we played outside'). • Links cause and effect and tells you what might happen next. • Talks about imaginary situations. • Uses language in role play. • Talks about feelings. • Develops a simple story. • Uses language to ask for information, to describe, to remember and to explain.

Evidence and progression notes

Area of Learning	Communication, Language and Literacy
Focus	Linking Sounds and Letters

	Development matters	Dates achieved	Examples
Birth – 11 months	• Listen to, distinguish and respond to intonations and the sounds of voices.		• Turns head towards a voice. • Watches your face and listens to your tone of voice with interest. • Is calmed by gentle words.

Evidence and progression notes

	Development matters	Dates achieved	Examples
8 – 20 months	• Enjoy babbling and increasingly experiment with using sounds and words to represent objects around them.		• Repeats strings of sounds when babbling (e.g. 'ma – ma – ma'). • Shouts to attract attention. • Turns to you when you call. • Makes a range of speech sounds.

Evidence and progression notes

	Development matters	Dates achieved	Examples
16 – 26 months	• Listen to and enjoy rhythmic patterns in rhymes and stories.		• Joins in a simple action rhyme. • Listens to and attempts favourite nursery rhymes. • Tries using rhythm.

Evidence and progression notes

© QEd Publications

Area of Learning	Communication, Language and Literacy
Focus	Linking Sounds and Letters

	Development matters	**Dates achieved**	**Examples**
22 – 36 months	• Distinguish one sound from another. • Show interest in play with sounds, songs and rhymes. • Repeat words or phrases from familiar stories.		• Says one or two words with meaning. • Asks for toys with sounds as well as gestures. • Listens to and enjoys rhymes and songs. • Uses six or more recognisable words. • Puts two words together. • Speaks in short phrases.

Evidence and progression notes

	Development matters	**Dates achieved**	**Examples**
30 – 50 months	• Enjoy rhyming and rhythmic activities. • Show awareness of rhyme and alliteration. • Recognise rhythm in spoken words.		• Uses tone and rhythm to add meaning. • Knows what a sound is even if it is out of sight (e.g. ambulance). • Repeats words or phrases in familiar stories. • Can clap the rhythm of their name. • Claps a familiar rhythm (e.g. Hickory Dickory Dock).

Evidence and progression notes

© QEd Publications

Area of Learning	Communication, Language and Literacy
Focus	Linking Sounds and Letters

	Development matters	Dates achieved	Examples
40 – 60 months	• Continue a rhyming string. • Hear and say the initial sound in words and know which letters represent some of the sounds. • **Hear and say sounds in words in the order in which they occur.** • **Link sounds to letters, naming and sounding the letters of the alphabet.** • **Use their phonic knowledge to write simple regular words and make phonetically plausible attempts at more complex words.**		• Can continue a rhyming string (e.g. when I was one I ate a ...). • Hears and says the first letter sound of their name. • Can listen to some letter sounds and point to the correct letter. • Can tell you the sound a word begins with when listening to simple words (e.g. dog). • Repeats the first sound of a word (e.g. car starts with 'c'). • Tells you words that rhyme with cat/toe/tree. • Can tell you the sound a word ends with when listening to simple words (e.g. tap). • Can repeat the short vowel sound in a word when listening to simple words (e.g. cat). • Blends letters to read CVC words and recognises common digraphs (e.g. 'br' 'sh'). • Hears and says sounds in words in the order in which they occur (ELG). • Links sounds to letters, naming and sounding the letters of the alphabet (ELG). • Uses phonic knowledge to write simple, regular words (c – a – t) (ELG).
Evidence and progression notes			

Area of Learning	Communication, Language and Literacy
Focus	Reading

	Development matters	Dates achieved	Examples
Birth – 11 months	• Listen to familiar sounds, words, or finger plays.		• Enjoys finger rhymes. • Looks briefly at pictures – one object per page. • Looks at pictures as adult turns pages. • Handles and explores a soft cover book.

Evidence and progression notes

	Development matters	Dates achieved	Examples
8 – 20 months	• Respond to words and interactive rhymes, such as 'Clap Hands'.		• Enjoys looking at pictures. • Responds to interactive games such as 'clap hands'. • Holds and looks at a picture book, attempting to turn pages.

Evidence and progression notes

© QEd Publications

Area of Learning	Communication, Language and Literacy
Focus	Reading

	Development matters	Dates achieved	Examples
16 – 26 months	• Show interest in stories, songs and rhymes.		• Looks at photographs with interest. • Holds picture book correctly and helps you turn pages. • Begins to handle books carefully.

Evidence and progression notes

	Development matters	Dates achieved	Examples
22 – 36 months	• Have some favourite stories, rhymes, songs, poems or jingles.		• Fetches a picture book to share with you. • Has a favourite book. • Begins to make links between a picture book and their surroundings.

Evidence and progression notes

© QEd Publications

Area of Learning	Communication, Language and Literacy
Focus	Reading

	Development matters	Dates achieved	Examples
30 – 50 months	• Listen to and join in with stories and poems, one-to-one and also in small groups. • Begin to be aware of the way stories are structured. • Suggest how the story might end. • Show interest in illustrations and print in books and print in the environment. • Handle books carefully. • Know information can be relayed in the form of print. • Hold books the correct way up and turn pages. • Understand the concept of a word.		• Listens to and joins in with stories in a small group. • Suggests what might happen next in a story. • Shares a picture book with another child. • Pretends to read a familiar picture book, remembering the broad details. • 'Reads' an unfamiliar picture book by making up a story based on the pictures. • Selects a card with their name on. • Shows an interest in print in the environment. • Knows what some familiar signs say or mean. • Begins to recognise some familiar words.
Evidence and progression notes			

© QEd Publications

Area of Learning	Communication, Language and Literacy
Focus	Reading

	Development matters	Dates achieved	Examples
40 – 60 months	- Enjoy an increasing range of books. - Know that information can be retrieved from books and computers. - **Explore and experiment with sounds, words and texts.** - **Retell narratives in the correct sequence, drawing on language patterns of stories.** - **Read a range of familiar and common words and simple sentences independently.** - **Know that print carries meaning and, in English, is read from left to right and top to bottom.** - **Show an understanding of the elements of stories, such as main character, sequence of events and openings, and how information can be found in non-fiction texts to answer questions about where, who, why and how.**		- Selects own books. - Has a favourite book and can tell you why. - Knows that books and computers tell you things. - Retells a simple story. - Can tell you the sound a word <u>begins</u> with when listening to simple words (e.g. <u>d</u>og). - Can tell you the sound a word <u>ends</u> with when listening to simple words (e.g. ta<u>p</u>). - Can repeat the short vowel sound in a word when listening to simple words (e.g. c<u>a</u>t). - Shows an understanding of the elements of stories – can tell you what happened at the beginning, middle and end. - Uses non-fiction books to find out information.

Evidence and progression notes

Area of Learning	Communication, Language and Literacy
Focus	Writing

	Development matters	Dates achieved	**Examples**
Birth – 11 months	• Move arms and legs and increasingly use them to reach for, grasp and manipulate things.		• Enjoys dabbling hands in water. • Plays with liquids on surfaces, e.g. puddles on the table.

Evidence and progression notes

	Development matters	Dates achieved	**Examples**
8 – 20 months	• Begin to make marks.		• Begins to make marks by dabbing or smearing. • Makes marks on paper.

Evidence and progression notes

	Development matters	Dates achieved	**Examples**
16 – 26 months	• Examine the marks they and others make.		• Makes patterns in the sand. • Repeats marks (e.g. strokes or rounds).

Evidence and progression notes

© QEd Publications

Area of Learning	Communication, Language and Literacy
Focus	Writing

	Development matters	Dates achieved	Examples
22 – 36 months	• Distinguish between the different marks they make.		• Repeats marks (e.g. strokes or rounds). • Scribbles boldly. • Pretends to write. • Attempts different letter shapes.

Evidence and progression notes

	Development matters	Dates achieved	Examples
30 – 50 months	• Sometimes give meaning to marks as they draw and paint. • Ascribe meanings to marks that they see in different places.		• Sometimes tell you that their marks mean words. • Draws a person. • Knows that some marks have meanings (e.g. what familiar logos mean, such as a favourite food chain). • Writes part of own name.

Evidence and progression notes

Area of Learning	Communication, Language and Literacy
Focus	Writing

	Development matters	**Dates achieved**	**Examples**
40 – 60 months	• Begin to break the flow of speech into words. • Use writing as a means of recording and communicating. • **Use their phonic knowledge to write simple regular words and make phonetically plausible attempts at more complex words.** • **Attempt writing for different purposes, using features of different forms such as lists, stories and instructions.** • Write their own names and other things such as labels and captions, and begin to form simple sentences, sometimes using punctuation.		• Dictates a simple phrase to you, breaking speech into separate words (e.g speaks slowly enough for an adult to write something down). • Tries writing a message. • Enjoys using written language in their play. • Makes a good attempt at writing a new word. • Uses knowledge of letter sounds to write a few simple, regular words (e.g. c – a – t).

Evidence and progression notes

Area of Learning	Communication, Language and Literacy
Focus	Handwriting

	Development matters	Dates achieved	Examples
Birth – 11 months	• Play with own fingers and toes and focus on objects around them.		• Plays with their fingers and toes. • Studies fingers carefully as they repeat patterns of movement.

Evidence and progression notes

	Development matters	Dates achieved	Examples
8 – 20 months	• Begin to bring together hand and eye movements to fix on and make contact with objects.		• Reaches for an object and secures it with their fingers. • Uses a poking movement in their play. • Holds small toys and strings.

Evidence and progression notes

© QEd Publications

Area of Learning	Communication, Language and Literacy
Focus	Handwriting

	Development matters	**Dates achieved**	**Examples**
16 – 26 months	• Make random marks with their fingers and some tools.		• Holds chunky crayons and scribbles freely. • Paints and dabs with better control.

Evidence and progression notes

	Development matters	**Dates achieved**	**Examples**
22 – 36 months	• Begin to show some control in their use of tools and equipment.		• Paints and dabs with better control. • Holds a chubby pencil between thumb and first two fingers.

Evidence and progression notes

Area of Learning	Communication, Language and Literacy
Focus	Handwriting

	Development matters	Dates achieved	Examples
30 – 50 months	• Use one-handed tools and equipment. • Draw lines and circles using gross motor movements. • Manipulate objects with increasing control.		• Makes large circular movement when painting. • Copies a vertical and horizontal line. • Traces over letter forms.

Evidence and progression notes

	Development matters	Dates achieved	Examples
40 – 60 months	• Begin to use anticlockwise movement and retrace vertical lines. • Begin to form recognisable letters. • **Use a pencil and hold it effectively to form recognisable letters, most of which are correctly formed.**		• Begins to make anticlockwise movements to make letter-like shapes. • Draws lines and circles. • Writes the first letter of their name. • Holds pencil correctly. • Forms many letters correctly. • Writes own first name.

Evidence and progression notes

© QEd Publications

General Observation and Planning Form

Activity	Comments	Member of staff/ parent/carer	Date

Area of Learning

Problem Solving, Reasoning and Numeracy

Aspects of Problem Solving, Reasoning and Numeracy

- Numbers as Labels and for Counting – how children gradually know and use numbers and counting in play, and eventually recognise and use numbers reliably, to develop mathematical ideas and to solve problems.

- Calculating – how children develop an awareness of the relationship between numbers and amounts and know that numbers can be combined to be 'added together' and can be separated by 'taking away' and that two or more amounts can be compared.

- Shape, Space and Measures – how through talking about shapes and quantities, and developing appropriate vocabulary, children use their knowledge to develop ideas and to solve mathematical problems.

from *The Early Years Foundation Stage* (DCFS, 2008)

Area of Learning	Problem Solving, Reasoning and Numeracy
Focus	Numbers as Labels and for Counting

	Development matters	Dates achieved	Examples
Birth – 11 months	• Respond to people and objects in their environment. • Notice changes in groupings of objects, images or sounds.		• Notices changes in how things are arranged around them (e.g. feeding time, changing or bathing time).

Evidence and progression notes

	Development matters	Dates achieved	Examples
8 – 20 months	• Develop an awareness of number names through their enjoyment of action rhymes and songs that relate to their experience of numbers. • Enjoy finding their nose, eyes or tummy as part of naming games.		• Enjoys number rhymes and naming games (e.g. eyes, nose and tummy). • Shows an interest when you counts steps.

Evidence and progression notes

	Development matters	Dates achieved	Examples
16 – 26 months	• Say some counting words randomly. • Distinguish between quantities, recognising that a group of objects is more than one. • Gain awareness of one-to-one correspondence through categorising belongings, starting with 'mine' or 'Mummy's'.		• Uses some number names spontaneously while playing. • Knows when things belong to someone (e.g. 'Daddy's'). • Shows curiosity in number symbols. • Joins in number rhymes and songs.

Evidence and progression notes

© QEd Publications

Area of Learning	Problem Solving, Reasoning and Numeracy
Focus	Numbers as Labels and for Counting

	Development matters	Dates achieved	**Examples**
22 – 36 months	• Have some understanding of 1 and 2, especially when the number is important for them. • Create and experiment with symbols and marks. • Use some number language, such as 'more' and 'a lot'. • Recite some number names in sequence.		• Experiments with symbols and marks. • Uses 'more' or 'lots' or 'all gone' in play. • Enjoys number activities. • Joins in when you count steps. • Uses marks or fingers to represent number.

Evidence and progression notes

	Development matters	Dates achieved	**Examples**
30 – 50 months	• Use some number names and number language spontaneously. • Show curiosity about numbers by offering comments or asking questions. • Use some number names accurately in play. • Sometimes match number and quantity correctly. • Recognise groups with one, two or three objects.		• Interested in the number relating to their age. • Identifies numerals '1', '2' or '3' when asked. • Joins in simple number rhymes. • Matches number and quantity. • Recognises groups with 1, 2 or 3 objects. • Can show you 'five fingers'. • Uses numbers in talk (e.g. 'Danny has 3').

Evidence and progression notes

© QEd Publications

Area of Learning	Problem Solving, Reasoning and Numeracy
Focus	Numbers as Labels and for Counting

	Development matters	Dates achieved	Examples
40 – 60 months	• Recognise some numerals of personal significance. • Count up to three or four objects by saying one number name for each item. • Count out up to six objects from a larger group. • Count actions or objects that cannot be moved. • Begin to count beyond 10. • Begin to represent numbers using fingers, marks on paper or pictures. • Select the correct numeral to represent 1 to 5, then 1 to 9 objects. • Recognise numerals 1 to 5. • Count an irregular arrangement of up to ten objects. • Estimate how many objects they can see and check by counting them. • Count aloud in ones, twos, fives or tens. • Know that numbers identify how many objects are in a set. • Use ordinal numbers in different contexts. • Match then compare the number of objects in two sets. • **Say and use number names in order in familiar contexts.** • **Count reliably up to ten everyday objects.** • **Recognise numerals 1 to 9.** • **Use developing mathematical ideas and methods to solve practical problems.**		• Begins to represent numbers by holding up correct number of fingers. • Selects numeral to represent 1 to 5 objects. • Arranges numerals 1 to 9 in correct sequence. • Selects correct numeral to represent 1 to 9 objects. • Knows that numbers identify how many objects are in a set. • Uses ordinal numbers in different contexts (e.g. first, second). • Counts out 5 objects with one-to-one correspondence. • Begins to count beyond 10. • Estimates how many objects they can see and checks by counting. • Counts aloud in ones, twos, fives or tens. • Matches then compares the number of objects in two sets. • Use language such as 'more' or 'less' to compare two numbers.

Evidence and progression notes

Area of Learning	Problem Solving, Reasoning and Numeracy
Focus	Calculating

	Development matters	Dates achieved	**Examples**
Birth – 11 months	• Are logical thinkers from birth.		• Enjoys 'peek-a-boo' games. • Enjoys handling small toys and shapes.

Evidence and progression notes

	Development matters	Dates achieved	**Examples**
8 – 20 months	• Have some understanding that things exist, even when out of sight. • Are alert to and investigate things that challenge their expectations.		• Knows that when you 'disappear' behind a screen you are still there. • Unwraps a hidden toy or present. • Fills and empties containers.

Evidence and progression notes

	Development matters	Dates achieved	**Examples**
16 – 26 months	• Are learning to classify by organising and arranging toys with increasing intent. • Categorise objects according to their properties.		• Begins to classify (e.g. line up cars together). • Matches objects by colour. • Orders two objects by height. • Orders three objects by length. • Can give you the 'big' one.

Evidence and progression notes

© QEd Publications

Area of Learning	Problem Solving, Reasoning and Numeracy
Focus	Calculating

	Development matters	Dates achieved	Examples
22 – 36 months	• Begin to make comparisons between quantities. • Know that a group of things changes in quantity when something is added or taken away.		• Begins to compare quantities in two sets. • Sorts objects into sets when playing (e.g. people and cars). • Begins to understand 'more' (e.g. notices another child has more red blocks).

Evidence and progression notes

	Development matters	Dates achieved	Examples
30 – 50 months	• Compare two groups of objects, saying when they have the same number. • Show an interest in number problems. • Separate a group of three or four objects in different ways, beginning to recognise that the total is still the same.		• Selects own category to sort into (e.g. sorts animals into sheep/pigs, into sizes or into colours). • Knows that one set becomes 'more' or 'less' if you add or take away things. • Can tell you if two sets have the 'same number' (1 to 5). • Orders three objects by weight/capacity. • Uses reasoning for solving practical problems (e.g. 'If I have three cups, I need three saucers').

Evidence and progression notes

© QEd Publications

Area of Learning	Problem Solving, Reasoning and Numeracy
Focus	Calculating

	Development matters	Dates achieved	Examples
40 – 60 months	<ul><li>Find the total number of items in two groups by counting all of them.</li><li>Use own methods to work through a problem.</li><li>Say the number that is one more than a given number.</li><li>Select two groups of objects to make a given total of objects.</li><li>Count repeated groups of the same size.</li><li>Share objects into equal groups and count how many in each group.</li><li>**In practical activities and discussion, begin to use the vocabulary involved in adding and subtracting.**</li><li>**Use language such as 'more' or 'less' to compare two numbers.**</li><li>**Find one more or one less than a number from one to ten.**</li><li>**Begin to relate addition to combining two groups of objects and subtraction to 'taking away'.**</li></ul>		<ul><li>Finds a grand total by counting two sets (e.g. adding a set of four bricks and three bricks).</li><li>Uses own methods to sort out a simple number problem.</li><li>Shares objects into equal groups.</li><li>Knows that 'adding' means combining groups together.</li><li>Knows that 'subtraction' is to do with taking away.</li><li>Finds one more or one less than a number from 1 to 10.</li></ul>

Evidence and progression notes

© QEd Publications

Area of Learning	Problem Solving, Reasoning and Numeracy
Focus	Shape, Space and Measures

	Development matters	Dates achieved	Examples
Birth – 11 months	• Develop an awareness of shape, form and texture as they encounter people and things in their environment.		• Watches a mobile as it twists and turns. • Shows interest in and stares at shapes (e.g. in a shape mobile). • Explores shapes and solids using touch and mouthing. • Crawls into their own space on the floor. • Enjoys playing with covers and blankets.

Evidence and progression notes

	Development matters	Dates achieved	Examples
8 – 20 months	• Find out what toys are like and can do through handling objects. • Recognise big things and small things in meaningful contexts.		• Shows interest in handling and exploring solid shapes. • Repeats movements in front of a mirror. • Arranges toys in spaces around them. • Plays with simple shape posting toy.

Evidence and progression notes

© QEd Publications

Area of Learning	Problem Solving, Reasoning and Numeracy
Focus	Shape, Space and Measures

	Development matters	**Dates achieved**	**Examples**
16 – 26 months	• Attempt, sometimes successfully, to fit shapes into spaces on inset boards or jigsaw puzzles. • Use blocks to create their own simple structures and arrangements. • Enjoy filling and emptying containers.		• Fits a shape into a posting box toy. • Fits a shape into an inset board. • Enjoys pouring water between big and little containers and uses this in simple problem solving.

Evidence and progression notes

	Development matters	**Dates achieved**	**Examples**
22 – 36 months	• Notice simple shapes and patterns in pictures. • Begin to categorise objects according to properties such as shape or size. • Are beginning to understand variations in size.		• Plays successfully with shape posting toys. • Begins to understand variations in size. • Enjoys simple inset boards and jigsaws. • Can fit stacking beakers on top of each other.

Evidence and progression notes

© QEd Publications

Area of Learning	Problem Solving, Reasoning and Numeracy
Focus	Shape, Space and Measures

	Development matters	Dates achieved	Examples
30 – 50 months	• Show an interest in shape and space by playing with shapes or making arrangements with objects. • Show awareness of similarities in shapes in the environment. • Observe and use positional language. • Are beginning to understand 'bigger than' and 'enough'. • Show interest in shape by sustained construction activity or by talking about shapes or arrangements. • Use shapes appropriately for tasks. • Begin to talk about the shapes of everyday objects.		• Recognises big things and small things in meaningful contexts. • Can show you which object is 'bigger than' or 'smaller than' another. • Sorts and matches simple shapes. • Follows simple directional cues (e.g. 'up' and 'down'). • Uses blocks in simple construction play.

Evidence and progression notes

© QEd Publications

Area of Learning	Problem Solving, Reasoning and Numeracy
Focus	Shape, Space and Measures

	Development matters	Dates achieved	Examples
40 – 60 months	• Show curiosity about and observation of shapes by talking about how they are the same or different. • Match some shapes by recognising similarities and orientation. • Begin to use mathematical names for 'solid' 3D shapes and 'flat' 2D shapes, and mathematical terms to describe shapes. • Select a particular named shape. • Show awareness of symmetry. • Find items from positional or directional clues. • Order two or three items by length or height. • Order two items by weight or capacity. • Match sets of objects to numerals that represent the number of objects. • Sort familiar objects to identify their similarities and differences, making choices and justifying decisions. • Describe solutions to practical problems, drawing on experience, talking about own ideas, methods and choices. • Use familiar objects and common shapes to create and recreate patterns and build models. • Use everyday language related to time; order and sequence familiar events, and measure short periods of time with a non-standard unit, for example, with a sand timer. • Count how many objects share a particular property, presenting results using pictures, drawings or numerals. • Count how many objects share a particular property, presenting results using pictures, drawings or numerals.		• Notices patterns around them and recreates these in their play or drawings. • Talks about the shapes of everyday objects. • Begins to use the names for 'solid' 3D shapes and 'flat' 2D shapes. • Works out which shape is needed to fit which space (e.g. in collage or designing). • Enjoys playing with tunnels and bridges, using positional language like 'over', 'under', 'in', 'on', 'behind', 'in front of'. • Follows simple directions such as 'here', 'there', 'on top' and 'through'. • Grades a set of objects by size. • Orders two items by length or height. • Measures a length by pacing it out. • Orders a group of children by height. • Enjoys using shapes in collage and talks about what they are doing. • Continues a given pattern with blocks/beads (e.g. red-yellow-red-yellow . . .). • Shows an understanding of spaces in their small world and imaginative play. • Talks about shapes and arrangements using words like 'circle', 'in a row', 'stripy'.

© QEd Publications

Area of Learning	Problem Solving, Reasoning and Numeracy
Focus	Shape, Space and Measures

	Development matters	Dates achieved	Examples
40 – 60 months continued	• Use language such as 'greater', 'smaller', 'heavier' or 'lighter' to compare quantities. • Talk about, recognise and recreate simple patterns. • Use language such as 'circle' or 'bigger' to describe the shape and size of solids and flat shapes. • Use everyday words to describe position. • Use developing mathematical ideas and methods to solve practical problems.		• Recognises and creates symmetry in their play, patterns and artwork (e.g. can make patterns on butterfly wings which are mirror images). • Uses a simple sand-timer to measure turn-taking. • Uses everyday language related to time. • Knows the sequence of events during a routine session.

Evidence and progression notes

General Observation and Planning Form

Activity	Comments	Member of staff/ parent/carer	Date

Area of Learning

Knowledge and Understanding of the World

Aspects of Knowledge and Understanding of the World

- Exploration and Investigation – how children investigate objects and materials and their properties, learn about change and patterns, similarities and differences, and question how and why things work.

- Designing and Making – ways in which children learn about the construction process, and tools and techniques that can be used to assemble materials creatively and safely.

- ICT – how children find out about and learn how to use appropriate information technology such as computers and programmable toys that support their learning.

- Time – how children find out about past and present events relevant to their own lives or those of their families.

- Place – how children become aware of and interested in the natural world, and find out about their local area, knowing what they like and dislike about it.

- Communities – how children begin to know about their own and other people's cultures in order to understand and celebrate the similarities and differences between them in a diverse society.

from The Early Years Foundation Stage (DCFS, 2008)

Area of Learning	Knowledge and Understanding of the World
Focus	Exploration and Investigation

	Development matters	**Dates achieved**	**Examples**
Birth – 11 months	• Use movement and senses to focus on, reach for and handle objects. • Learn by observation about actions and their effects.		• Watches movement of own hand in front of face. • Enjoys objects and playthings through shaking, banging and mouthing. • Enjoys watching colours or lights. • Enjoys crumpling or tearing paper.

Evidence and progression notes

	Development matters	**Dates achieved**	**Examples**
8 – 20 months	• As they pull to stand and become more mobile, the scope of babies' investigations widens.		• Crawls towards a colourful ball. • Pulls self along the furniture to reach new objects of interest. • Explores and investigates playthings by putting in and emptying out. • Enjoys splashing with water.

Evidence and progression notes

© QEd Publications

Area of Learning	Knowledge and Understanding of the World
Focus	Exploration and Investigation

	Development matters	Dates achieved	Examples
16 – 26 months	• Sometimes focus their enquiries on particular features or processes.		• Copies facial expressions (e.g. looks serious when adult does). • Copies hand clapping. • Copies adult doing routine things. • Assembles a simple train track or road layout. • Matches objects (e.g. a lid for a teapot).

Evidence and progression notes

	Development matters	Dates achieved	Examples
22 – 36 months	• Explore, play and seek meaning in their experiences. • Use others as sources of information and learning. • Show an interest in why things happen.		• Shows an interest in new activities. • Asks others why things happen. • Shows sign of forward planning (e.g. looks for coat when adult says it's outdoor play). • Explores which things sink or float. • Explores which things roll.

Evidence and progression notes

© QEd Publications

Area of Learning	Knowledge and Understanding of the World
Focus	Exploration and Investigation

	Development matters	Dates achieved	Examples
30 – 50 months	• Show curiosity and interest in the features of objects and living things. • Describe and talk about what they see. • Show curiosity about why things happen and how things work. • Show understanding of cause/effect relations.		• Looks inside/behind to see how things work. • Examines objects and living things to find out more. • Describes and talks about what they see and hear. • Asks 'what' and 'why' questions, showing an awareness of change.

Evidence and progression notes

	Development matters	Dates achieved	Examples
40 – 60 months	• Notice and comment on patterns. • Show an awareness of change. • Explain own knowledge and understanding, and ask appropriate questions of others. • **Investigate objects and materials by using all of their senses as appropriate.** • **Find out about, and identify, some features of living things, objects and events they observe.** • **Look closely at similarities, differences, patterns and change.** • **Ask questions about why things happen and how things work.**		• Interested in new activities and keen to experience and explore them. • Finds out what a seed needs in order to grow. • Notices and is interested in weather changes. • Asks questions about the natural world. • Looks up information in a non-fiction picture book. • Makes links between their talking, doing and finding out through books or ICT.

Evidence and progression notes

Area of Learning	Knowledge and Understanding of the World
Focus	Designing and Making

	Development matters	**Dates achieved**	**Examples**
Birth – 11 months	• Explore objects and materials using hand and mouth.		• Explores objects using mouthing and touch. • Enjoys handling small toys.

Evidence and progression notes

	Development matters	**Dates achieved**	**Examples**
8 – 20 months	• Show curiosity and interest in things that are built up and fall down, and that open and close.		• Enjoys watching when you stack bricks and knock them down. • Fills and empties containers. • Curious about containers that open and close.

Evidence and progression notes

© QEd Publications

Area of Learning	Knowledge and Understanding of the World
Focus	Designing and Making

	Development matters	Dates achieved	Examples
16 – 26 months	• Are interested in pushing and pulling things, and begin to build structures.		• Looks inside a simple container in order to find the contents. • Plays with push-along toys. • Walks pulling a wheeled toy on a cord.

Evidence and progression notes

	Development matters	Dates achieved	Examples
22 – 36 months	• Are curious and interested in making things happen.		• Builds a tower of 3 to 5 bricks. • Joins construction pieces together to build and balance. • Moulds wet sand. • Makes simple models/patterns with construction toys.

Evidence and progression notes

© QEd Publications

Area of Learning	Knowledge and Understanding of the World
Focus	Designing and Making

	Development matters	Dates achieved	Examples
30 – 50 months	• Investigate various construction materials. • Realise tools can be used for a purpose. • Join construction pieces together to build and balance. • Begin to try out a range of tools and techniques safely.		• Sustains play with blocks and construction pieces. • Uses large cartons to construct a den. • Fits together interlocking construction bricks to make something. • Uses simple tools with play dough (e.g. to make holes, shapes etc). • Uses simple tools with supervision and support.

Evidence and progression notes

	Development matters	Dates achieved	Examples
40 – 60 months	• Construct with a purpose in mind, using a variety of resources. • Use simple tools and techniques competently and appropriately. • **Build and construct with a wide range of objects, selecting appropriate resources and adapting their work where necessary.** • **Select the tools and techniques they need to shape, assemble and join materials they are using.**		• Explores different techniques for constructing (e.g. gluing, stacking, interlocking). • Uses a range of simple tools safely (e.g. scissors, glue sticks, cleaning cloth). • Copies a simple design (e.g. a stairway of bricks). • Designs and makes a simple track layout (e.g. train track). • Can plan, construct and then review what has been made.

Evidence and progression notes

© QEd Publications

Area of Learning	Knowledge and Understanding of the World
Focus	ICT

	Development matters	**Dates achieved**	**Examples**
Birth – 11 months	• Shows interest in toys and resources that incorporate technology.		• Interested in play telephones and computer/TV screens. • Shows interest in objects (e.g. bear that makes a noise when you turn it over, rattles etc).

Evidence and progression notes

	Development matters	**Dates achieved**	**Examples**
8 – 20 months	• Explore things with interest and sometimes press parts or lift flaps to achieve effects such as sounds, movements or new images.		• Interested in buttons, knobs and dials on activity centre toys. • Enjoys lift-the-flap books, pop up toys.

Evidence and progression notes

	Development matters	**Dates achieved**	**Examples**
16 – 26 months	• Show interest in toys with buttons and flaps and simple mechanisms and begin to learn to operate them.		• Pretends to use the phone or simple camera. • Links cause with effect (e.g. playing with a pop-up toy).

Evidence and progression notes

© QEd Publications

Area of Learning	Knowledge and Understanding of the World
Focus	ICT

	Development matters	Dates achieved	**Examples**
22 – 36 months	• Show an interest in ICT. • Seek to acquire basic skills in turning on and operating some ICT equipment.		• Knows what simple ICT equipment can do. • Interested and curious about ICT. • Operates a simple touch pad or switch.

Evidence and progression notes

	Development matters	Dates achieved	**Examples**
30 – 50 months	• Know how to operate simple equipment.		• Knows how to operate simple equipment (e.g. turning a knob). • Can select and take a photograph with a digital camera. • Begins to use everyday technology (knows what a torch or radio or computer can be used for).

Evidence and progression notes

	Development matters	Dates achieved	**Examples**
40 – 60 months	• Complete a simple program on a computer. • Use ICT to perform simple functions, such as selecting a channel on the TV remote control. • Use a mouse and keyboard to interact with age-appropriate computer software. • **Find out about and identify the uses of everyday technology and use information and communication technology and programmable toys to support their learning.**		• Can take part in a simple computer learning game. • Uses technology (e.g. a remote control, a CD player). • Begins to use a computer mouse, linking cause with effect. • Starts to use a telephone.

Evidence and progression notes

© QEd Publications

Area of Learning	Knowledge and Understanding of the World
Focus	Time

	Development matters	**Dates achieved**	**Examples**
Birth – 11 months	• Anticipate repeated sounds, sights and actions.		• Anticipates what is about to happen (e.g. seeing their bottle, their mobile, splashing in water, baby massage sessions).

Evidence and progression notes

	Development matters	**Dates achieved**	**Examples**
8 – 20 months	• Get to know and enjoy daily routines, such as getting-up time, mealtimes, nappy time, and bedtime.		• Follows familiar routines. • Waves bye bye. • Gets settled for a sleep. • Anticipates and cooperates at mealtimes and changing times.

Evidence and progression notes

© QEd Publications

Area of Learning	Knowledge and Understanding of the World
Focus	Time

	Development matters	Dates achieved	Examples
16 – 26 months	• Associate a sequence of actions with daily routines. • Begin to understand that things might happen 'now'.		• Joins in familiar routines such as putting a coat on to go outside. • Anticipates an action in a familiar rhyme. • Shows through role-play that they can follow simple routines and sequences.

Evidence and progression notes

	Development matters	Dates achieved	Examples
22 – 36 months	• Recognise some special times in their lives and the lives of others. • Understand some talk about immediate past and future, for example, 'before', 'later' or 'soon'. • Anticipate specific time-based events such as mealtimes or home time.		• Recognises some special times in their life. • Talks about what is happening. • Shares special times in others' lives. • Arranges photographs of a simple sequence of actions in order (e.g. getting up in the morning).

Evidence and progression notes

© QEd Publications

Area of Learning	Knowledge and Understanding of the World
Focus	Time

	Development matters	Dates achieved	**Examples**
30 – 50 months	• Remember and talk about significant events in their own experience. • Show interest in the lives of people familiar to them. • Talk about past and future events. • Develop an understanding of growth, decay and changes over time.		• Talks about tomorrow or yesterday. • Makes connections between their play and their experiences (e.g. 'This is how Dad does it at home'). • Tells you about things they remember from before (e.g. when they were 'little'). • Talks about photographs of when they were younger. • Can predict what might happen next.

Evidence and progression notes

	Development matters	Dates achieved	**Examples**
40 – 60 months	• Begin to differentiate between past and present. • Use time-related words in conversation. • Understand about the seasons of the year and their regularity. • Make short-term future plans. • **Find out about past and present events in their own lives, and in those of their families and other people they know.**		• Uses talk to describe a sequence of events. • Can begin to talk to you about what happened in their past and what is present. • Uses words related to time in conversation. • Understands about the changing seasons of the year. • Makes plans for the near future.

Evidence and progression notes

Area of Learning	Knowledge and Understanding of the World
Focus	Place

	Development matters	Dates achieved	Examples
Birth – 11 months	• Explore the space around them through movements of hands and feet and by rolling.		• Moves arms and legs around to explore the place around them. • Creeps, rolls or crawls into new places.

Evidence and progression notes

	Development matters	Dates achieved	Examples
8 – 20 months	• Love to be outdoors and closely observe what animals, people and vehicles do.		• Enjoys the outside and all that can be seen and heard there. • Enjoys watching animals and pets, commenting with words and actions.

Evidence and progression notes

© QEd Publications

Area of Learning	Knowledge and Understanding of the World
Focus	Place

	Development matters	Dates achieved	**Examples**
16 – 26 months	• Are curious about the environment.		• Shows curiosity about their environment (e.g. warmth of the sun, insects, puddles, windy weather, flowers etc).

Evidence and progression notes

	Development matters	Dates achieved	**Examples**
22 – 36 months	• Enjoy playing with small-world models such as a farm, a garage, or a train track.		• Enjoys small-world play such as farms and garages. • Able to extend small-world play by adding new ideas.

Evidence and progression notes

© QEd Publications

Area of Learning	Knowledge and Understanding of the World
Focus	Place

	Development matters	Dates achieved	**Examples**
30 – 50 months	• Show an interest in the world in which they live. • Comment and ask questions about where they live and the natural world.		• Interested to explore more about the world through books or ICT. • Asks questions about what is going on around them. • Talks about other places not in the 'here and now' such as their home or holiday.

Evidence and progression notes

	Development matters	Dates achieved	**Examples**
40 – 60 months	• Notice differences between features of the local environment. • Observe, find out about and identify features in the place they live and the natural world. • Find out about their environment, and talk about those features they like and dislike.		• Able to recreate features of the built environment in their models or art. • Notices differences between features of the local environment (e.g. 'There's a new traffic light'). • Finds out about events they experience (e.g 'Why do we need to go to the dentist?').

Evidence and progression notes

© QEd Publications

Area of Learning	Knowledge and Understanding of the World
Focus	Communities

	Development matters	**Dates achieved**	**Examples**
Birth – 11 months	• Concentrate intently on faces and enjoy interaction. • Form attachments to special people.		• Turns eyes towards person talking. • Focuses intently on the faces around them. • Snuggles in when held. • Shows pleasure in being amongst others.

Evidence and progression notes

	Development matters	**Dates achieved**	**Examples**
8 – 20 months	• Recognise special people, such as family, friends or their key person. • Show interest in social life around them.		• Recognises familiar and special people (e.g. family, friends, key person). • Appears to feel safe and secure in the group.

Evidence and progression notes

© QEd Publications

Area of Learning	Knowledge and Understanding of the World
Focus	Communities

	Development matters	**Dates achieved**	**Examples**
16 – 26 months	• Are curious about people and show interest in stories about themselves and their family. • Enjoy stories about themselves, their families and other people. • Like to play alongside other children.		• Enjoys looking at a photograph album of self and their family. • Knows the names of some children in the setting. • Likes to have a familiar adult nearby. • Seeks out others to share experiences.

Evidence and progression notes

	Development matters	**Dates achieved**	**Examples**
22 – 36 months	• Are interested in others and their families. • Have a sense of own immediate family and relations. • Begin to have their own friends.		• Interested to hear about other children's lives and news. • Talks about who their friends are. • Knows the names of many children in the setting. • Plays with a group of children in the home corner.

Evidence and progression notes

Area of Learning	Knowledge and Understanding of the World
Focus	Communities

	Development matters	Dates achieved	Examples
30 – 50 months	• Express feelings about a significant personal event. • Describe significant events for family or friends. • Enjoy imaginative and role-play with peers. • Show interest in different occupations and ways of life.		• Expresses their feelings about a significant personal event. • Tells parents or carers about what they have done in the group. • Talks about significant events at home to members of the group (e.g. a wedding, birthday). • Talks about where they live and their local community. • Talks about different jobs people do (e.g. fireman, shopkeeper, hairdresser).

Evidence and progression notes

	Development matters	Dates achieved	Examples
40 – 60 months	• Gain an awareness of the cultures and beliefs of others. • Feel a sense of belonging to own community and place. • **Begin to know about their own cultures and beliefs and those of other people.**		• Has an awareness of and talks about similarities and differences in others. • Talks about neighbours neighbourhood and close friends. • Has an awareness of the cultures and beliefs of others.

Evidence and progression notes

© QEd Publications

General Observation and Planning Form

Activity	Comments	Member of staff/ parent/carer	Date

Area of Learning

Physical Development

Aspects of Physical Development

- Movement and Space – how children learn to move with confidence, imagination and safety, with an awareness of space, themselves and others.

- Health and Bodily Awareness – how children learn the importance of keeping healthy and the factors that contribute to maintaining their health.

- Using Equipment and Materials – ways in which children use a range of small and large equipment.

from *The Early Years Foundation Stage* (DCFS, 2008)

Area of Learning	Physical Development
Focus	Movement and Space

	Development matters	**Dates achieved**	**Examples**
Birth – 11 months	• Make movements with arms and legs which gradually become more controlled. • Use movement and sensory exploration to link up with their immediate environment.		• Raises arms to bottle • Uses arms and legs to make contact with things around them. • Watches movement of own hand in front of face.

Evidence and progression notes

	Development matters	**Dates achieved**	**Examples**
8 – 20 months	• Make strong and purposeful movements, often moving from the position in which they are placed. • Use their increasing mobility to connect with toys, objects and people. • Show delight in the freedom and changing perspectives that standing or beginning to walk brings.		• Able to move away from the position they are placed in. • Kicks and waves arms to music. • Crawls over rugs and cushions. • Loves to creep, crawl or shuffle. • Creeps or crawls towards something of interest. • Picks up a small toy.

Evidence and progression notes

© QEd Publications

Area of Learning	Physical Development
Focus	Movement and Space

	Development matters	Dates achieved	Examples
16 – 26 months	• Have a biological drive to use their bodies and develop their physical skills. • Express themselves through action and sound. • Are excited by their own increasing mobility and often set their own challenges.		• Enjoys holding on to a hand or piece of furniture and 'bouncing'. • Toddles from one person to another (5 – 6 steps). • Toddles at speed, using voice while moving. • Rolls ball between adult and self. • Walks across the room. • Responds to sound with body movements.

Evidence and progression notes

	Development matters	Dates achieved	Examples
22 – 36 months	• Gradually gain control of their whole bodies and are becoming aware of how to negotiate the space and objects around them. • Move spontaneously within available space. • Respond to rhythm, music and story by means of gesture and movement. • Are able to stop. • Manage body to create intended movements. • Combine and repeat a range of movements.		• Walks backwards. • Finds three different ways of moving across a room (e.g. walking, jumping, crawling). • Begins to show increasing control (e.g. jump, kick a ball, balance briefly on one leg). • Avoids bumping into/treading over others. • Finds own space on a crowded floor. • Dances to music.

Evidence and progression notes

© QEd Publications

Area of Learning	Physical Development
Focus	Movement and Space

	Development matters	Dates achieved	Examples
30 – 50 months	• Move freely with pleasure and confidence in a range of ways, such as slithering, shuffling, rolling, crawling, walking, running, jumping, skipping, sliding and hopping. • Use movement to express feelings. • Negotiate space successfully when playing racing and chasing games with other children, adjusting speed or changing direction to avoid obstacles. • Sit up, stand up and balance on various parts of the body. • Demonstrate the control necessary to hold a shape or fixed position. • Operate equipment by means of pushing and pulling movements. • Mount stairs, steps or climbing equipment using alternate feet. • Negotiate an appropriate pathway when walking, running or using a wheelchair or other mobility aids, both indoors and outdoors. • Judge body space in relation to spaces available when fitting into confined spaces or negotiating openings and boundaries. • Show respect for other children's personal space when playing among them. • Persevere in repeating some actions or attempts when developing a new skill. • Collaborate in devising and sharing tasks, including those which involve accepting rules.		• Moves freely and confidently (e.g. rolling, running, jumping, hopping). • Performs a range of movements imaginatively (e.g. squirming, twisting, walking on tiptoe). • Runs and changes direction to avoid obstacles. • Shows balance when playing (e.g. creeping, tiptoeing, bunny hopping). • Throws a ball with approximate aim. • Begins to operate equipment (e.g. a computer mouse with a simple game). • Climbs up steps to slide or onto climbing frame. • Attempts range of movements on a climbing frame (e.g. climbing around, under, over, through). • Makes repeated attempts at a new skill. • Accepts simple rules in a game of 'catch me' or ball kicking.

Evidence and progression notes

Area of Learning	Physical Development
Focus	Movement and Space

	Development matters	Dates achieved	**Examples**
40 – 60 months	• Go backwards and sideways as well as forwards. • Experiment with different ways of moving. • Initiate new combinations of movement and gesture in order to express and respond to feelings, ideas and experiences. • Jump off an object and land appropriately. • Show understanding of the need for safety when tackling new challenges. • Avoid dangerous places and equipment. • Construct with large materials such as cartons, fabric and planks. • **Move with confidence, imagination and in safety.** • **Move with control and coordination.** • **Travel around, under, over and through balancing and climbing equipment.** • **Show awareness of space, of themselves and of others.**		• Makes full and safe use of the climbing frame. • Moves backwards and sideways as well as forwards. • Marches to a steady rhythm. • Tries new ideas for moving (e.g. when dancing). • Jumps from a step and land safely. • Shows awareness of the need for safety (e.g. walks carefully when carrying scissors). • Manages own buttons and zips. • Threads large beads and stack small blocks. • Shows preference for one hand consistently. • Handles construction materials with increasing control (cartons, planks, interlocking bricks).

Evidence and progression notes

Area of Learning	Physical Development
Focus	Health and Bodily Awareness

	Development matters	Dates achieved	Examples
Birth – 11 months	• Thrive when their nutritional needs are met. • Respond to and thrive on warm, sensitive physical contact and care.		• Feeds at regular intervals throughout the day. • Puts hands on bottle when feeding. • Snuggles in with pleasure when cuddled.

Evidence and progression notes

	Development matters	Dates achieved	Examples
8 – 20 months	• Need rest and sleep, as well as food. • Focus on what they want as they begin to crawl, pull to stand, creep, shuffle, walk or climb.		• Lets you know when they need a rest. • Turns face away to show dislike of certain foods. • Tugs at wet or dirty nappy.

Evidence and progression notes

© QEd Publications

Area of Learning	Physical Development
Focus	Health and Bodily Awareness

	Development matters	Dates achieved	Examples
16 – 26 months	• Show some awareness of bladder and bowel urges. • Develop their own likes and dislikes in food, drink and activity. • Practise and develop what they can do.		• Indicates when toilet is needed with some accidents. • Indicates choice at meal and snack times. • Helps to wash and dry own hands.

Evidence and progression notes

	Development matters	Dates achieved	Examples
22 – 36 months	• Communicate their needs for things such as food, drinks and when they are uncomfortable. • Show emerging autonomy in self-care.		• Lets you know when they need something (e.g. nappy change, a drink when thirsty). • Sometimes able to use a potty/toilet with reminders. • Dry by day.

Evidence and progression notes

© QEd Publications

Area of Learning	Physical Development
Focus	Health and Bodily Awareness

	Development matters	Dates achieved	Examples
30 – 50 months	• Show awareness of own needs with regard to eating, sleeping and hygiene. • Often need adult support to meet those needs. • Show awareness of a range of healthy practices with regard to eating, sleeping and hygiene. • Observe the effects of activity on their bodies.		• Able to control bowels. • Feeds self with a spoon and fork. • Shows awareness of own needs (e.g. needing a tissue to wipe nose). • Asks for drinks and food when they need them. • Can tell you what happens to their body after they have been running. • Washes hands after using the toilet.

Evidence and progression notes

	Development matters	Dates achieved	Examples
40 – 60 months	• Show some understanding that good practices with regard to exercise, eating, sleeping and hygiene can contribute to good health. • **Recognise the importance of keeping healthy, and those things which contribute to this.** • **Recognise the changes that happen to their bodies when they are active.**		• Can tell you why they need a good sleep at night. • Shows an awareness of good habits (e.g. washing hands before eating, throwing away used tissues). • Observes what changes when their body becomes active (e.g. feeling 'puffed', getting warm).

Evidence and progression notes

© QEd Publications

Area of Learning	Physical Development
Focus	Using Equipment and Materials

	Development matters	Dates achieved	Examples
Birth – 11 months	• Watch and explore hands and feet. • Reach out for, touch and begin to hold objects.		• Plays with own fists and feet. • Explores objects with mouth. • Holds rattle for a couple of seconds when placed in palm of hand. • Starts to reach out to toys or objects. • Enjoys handling small toys (banging, shaking, turning, passing from hand to hand). • Holds two toys, one in each hand.

Evidence and progression notes

	Development matters	Dates achieved	Examples
8 – 20 months	• Imitate and improvise actions they have observed, such as clapping and waving. • Become absorbed in putting objects in and out of containers. • Enjoy the sensory experience of making marks in damp sand, paste or paint. This is particularly important for babies who have a visual impairment.		• Copies raising both hands in the air. • Imitates hand clapping. • Fills and empties containers (e.g. shape posting toys, pop-up toys, putting one thing inside the other). • Uses a pointing finger to indicate things. • Enjoys manipulating sand or play dough. • Buries and finds toys in the sand. • Pokes with one finger.

Evidence and progression notes

Area of Learning	Physical Development
Focus	Using Equipment and Materials

	Development matters	Dates achieved	Examples
16 – 26 months	• Use tools and materials for particular purposes. • Begin to make, and manipulate, objects and tools. • Put together a sequence of actions.		• Enjoys handling collage material. • Dabs with a glue stick. • Sticks one craft piece to another. • Rolls out malleable materials. • Pokes and makes marks in wet sand with a simple tool. • Snips with scissors. • Turns a simple dial/screwtop.

Evidence and progression notes

	Development matters	Dates achieved	Examples
22 – 36 months	• Balance blocks to create simple structures. • Show increasing control in holding and using hammers, books, beaters and mark-making tools.		• Stacks blocks to make a tower. • Can fit stacking beakers on top of each other. • Can complete a simple six-piece jigsaw. • Uses molds and templates to form and shape materials. • Shows increasing control (e.g. operate a hammer and peg toy, eating with spoon and fork). • Pushes and pulls wheeled toys.

Evidence and progression notes

Area of Learning	Physical Development
Focus	Using Equipment and Materials

	Development matters	Dates achieved	Examples
30 – 50 months	• Engage in activities requiring hand-eye coordination. • Use one-handed tools and equipment. • Show increasing control over clothing and fastenings. • Show increasing control in using equipment for climbing, scrambling, sliding and swinging. • Demonstrate increasing skill and control in the use of mark-making implements, blocks, construction sets and small-world activities. • Understand that equipment and tools have to be used safely.		• Carefully handles and manipulates 'small world' objects such as farm animals and toy cars. • Cuts along a straight line with scissors. • Uses a computer mouse with a simple game. • Swings, slides and climbs safely. • Enjoys small world play in wet or dry sand with increasing control and detail. • Understands the need for safety (e.g. know that spills need cleaning up). • Tidies up a familiar area independently. • Retrieves, collects and catches a selection of balls.

Evidence and progression notes

Area of Learning	Physical Development
Focus	Using Equipment and Materials

	Development matters	Dates achieved	Examples
40 – 60 months	• Explore malleable materials by patting, stroking, poking, squeezing, pinching and twisting them. • Use increasing control over an object, such as a ball, by touching, pushing, patting, throwing, catching or kicking it. • Manipulate materials to achieve a planned effect. • Use simple tools to effect changes to the materials. • Show understanding of how to transport and store equipment safely. • Practise some appropriate safety measures without direct supervision. • **Use a range of small and large equipment.** • **Handle tools, objects, construction and malleable materials safely and with increasing control.**		• Manipulates materials to achieve a planned effect (e.g. building a 'lorry', forms clay into sausages). • Uses simple tools to effect changes in materials (e.g. use a hammer safely when woodworking). • Cuts out a simple shape. • Explains why we need to handle tools safely (e.g. when using a hammer). • Takes some simple safety precautions without reminding (e.g. walks carefully when carrying scissors). • Knows which tools to use for different materials (e.g. in the woodworking corner). • Builds model from interlocking bricks.

Evidence and progression notes

General Observation and Planning Form

Activity	Comments	Member of staff/ parent/carer	Date

Area of Learning

Creative Development

Aspects of Creative Development

- Being Creative – Responding to Experiences, Expressing and Communicating Ideas – how children respond in a variety of ways to what they see, hear, smell, touch or feel and how, as a result of these encounters, they express and communicate their own ideas, thoughts and feelings.

- Exploring Media and Materials – finding out about, thinking about and working with colour, texture, shape, space and form in two and three dimensions.

- Creating Music and Dance – how sounds can be made and changed and how sounds can be recognised and repeated from a pattern . . . ways of exploring movement, matching movements to music and singing simple songs from memory.

- Developing Imagination and Imaginative Play – how children are supported to develop and build their imaginations through stories, role-play, imaginative play, dance, music, design and art.

from *The Early Years Foundation Stage* (DCFS, 2008)

Area of Learning	Creative Development
Focus	Being Creative – Responding to Experiences, Expressing & Communicating Ideas

	Development matters	Dates achieved	**Examples**
Birth – 11 months	• Use movement and sensory exploration to connect with their immediate environment.		• Accompanies movements with voice and sound. • Uses a range of methods to communicate how they are feeling (e.g. hand waving, gurgling, copying facial expressions). • Stops fretting when soft music is played.
Evidence and progression notes			

	Development matters	Dates achieved	**Examples**
8 – 20 months	• Respond to what they see, hear, smell, touch and feel.		• Startled by sudden, loud noise. • Echoes a sound (e.g. 'ba-ba'). • Looks for fallen toy. • Shows an interest in what they touch and feel (e.g. splash in water or manipulate sand).
Evidence and progression notes			

© QEd Publications

Area of Learning	Creative Development
Focus	Being Creative – Responding to Experiences, Expressing & Communicating Ideas

	Development matters	**Dates achieved**	**Examples**
16 – 26 months	• Express themselves through physical action and sound. • Explore by repeating patterns of play.		• Quietens and can focus when listening carefully. • Repeats patterns of play over and over. • Repeats actions in order to explore what effect something has. • Happy to explore an activity or object with someone else. • Calls out for someone to look at something they have seen. • Looks up at you as they play or create something. • Shows you what they have done.

Evidence and progression notes

	Development matters	**Dates achieved**	**Examples**
22 – 36 months	• Seek to make sense of what they see, hear, smell, touch and feel. • Begin to use representation as a form of communication.		• Makes noises to music. • Pats a drum or tambourine. • Begins to differentiate colours when painting. • Makes comments about smells. • Begins to use representation to communicate what they feel (e.g. jumping for excitement).

Evidence and progression notes

© QEd Publications

Area of Learning	Creative Development
Focus	Being Creative – Responding to Experiences, Expressing & Communicating Ideas

	Development matters	Dates achieved	Examples
30 – 50 months	• Use language and other forms of communication to share the things they create, or to indicate personal satisfaction or frustration. • Explore and experience using a range of senses and movement. • Capture experiences and responses with music, dance, paint and other materials or words. • Develop preferences for forms of expression.		• Talks about the things they have made/drawn/painted. • Uses art or craft to represent an experience (e.g. a holiday). • Paints a picture to represent how they feel (e.g. a 'happy' picture). • Tells you how they feel about their creation. • Shows you how they feel through art and craft. • Shows a preference about how they like to express themselves (e.g. voice/music/dance/art).

Evidence and progression notes

Area of Learning	Creative Development
Focus	Being Creative – Responding to Experiences, Expressing & Communicating Ideas

	Development matters	Dates achieved	Examples
40 – 60 months	• Talk about personal intentions, describing what they were trying to do. • Respond to comments and questions, entering into dialogue about their creations. • Make comparisons and create new connections. • **Respond in a variety of ways to what they see, hear, smell, touch and feel.** • **Express and communicate their ideas, thoughts and feelings by using a widening range of materials, suitable tools, imaginative and role-play, movement, designing and making, and a variety of songs and musical instruments.**		• Plans a creation ahead (e.g. 'I want to make a shiny, blue sea picture'). • Tries to capture experiences with materials (e.g. a sea collage with sand, shells and blue cellophane) and talks about what they are trying to do. • Interacts with others, talking about what they have made and listening to others' suggestions. • Expresses their feelings using designing and making (e.g. 'I like this because …'). • Makes comparisons and creates new connections (e.g. make a connection between fireworks and being cold; different music makes you feel different).

Evidence and progression notes

Area of Learning	Creative Development
Focus	Exploring Media and Materials

	Development matters	**Dates achieved**	**Examples**
Birth – 11 months	• Discover mark-making by chance, noticing, for instance, that trailing a finger through spilt juice changes it.		• Enjoys watching colours or lights. • Enjoys crumpling and tearing paper. • Enjoys the bubbles in a bath.

Evidence and progression notes

	Development matters	**Dates achieved**	**Examples**
8 – 20 months	• Explore and experiment with a range of media using whole body.		• Enjoys handling collage material. • Shows early mark-making when playing with food and spills. • Enjoys playing with paint, dough, bubbles and making marks on paper.

Evidence and progression notes

© QEd Publications

Area of Learning	Creative Development
Focus	Exploring Media and Materials

	Development matters	**Dates achieved**	**Examples**
16 – 26 months	• Create and experiment with blocks, colour and marks.		• Dabs with a glue stick. • Creates simple patterns and structures using blocks. • Arranges and rearranges their food and playthings. • Enjoys finger painting and hand prints.

Evidence and progression notes

	Development matters	**Dates achieved**	**Examples**
22 – 36 months	• Begin to combine movement, materials, media or marks.		• Begins to apply colours or paints to different surfaces. • Enjoys painting with a brush. • Snips with scissors.

Evidence and progression notes

© QEd Publications

Area of Learning	Creative Development
Focus	Exploring Media and Materials

	Development matters	Dates achieved	**Examples**
30 – 50 months	• Begin to be interested in and describe the texture of things. • Explore colour and begin to differentiate between colours. • Differentiate marks and movements on paper. • Use their bodies to explore texture and space. • Understand that they can use lines to enclose a space, and then begin to use these shapes to represent objects. • Create 3D structures. • Begin to construct, stacking blocks vertically and horizontally, making enclosures and creating spaces.		• Shows interest in different textures (e.g. makes comparisons between materials using words like 'smooth', 'shiny', 'soft', 'hard', 'light', 'heavy'). • Explores colour and begins to match and sort by colour. • Chooses colours to use for a purpose (e.g. fiery colours for the bonfire). • Explores lines and shapes (e.g. paints a recognisable 'person' or a 'house'). • Begins to construct 3D shapes (e.g. a model out of boxes). • Begins to make enclosures (e.g. a den using blankets and boxes).

Evidence and progression notes

Area of Learning	Creative Development
Focus	Exploring Media and Materials

	Development matters	Dates achieved	Examples
40 – 60 months	- Explore what happens when they mix colours. - Choose particular colours to use for a purpose. - Understand that different media can be combined to create new effects. - Experiment to create different textures. - Create constructions, collages, painting and drawings. - Use ideas involving fitting, overlapping, in, out, enclosure, grids and sun-like shapes. - Work creatively on a large or small scale. - **Explore colour, texture, shape, form and space in two or three dimensions.**		- Tries different media to create new effects (e.g. a collage using paper, sand, fabric, pasta). - Experiments to create different textures (e.g. puts glue on sawdust). - Creates paintings and drawings. - Selects the best materials for the job (e.g. to make a strong bridge). - Creates constructions and collages. - Uses ideas involving fitting, overlapping, in and out in their 3D creations using objects with different textures (e.g. feathery, lacy). - Uses ideas involving stripes, enclosures, grids and sunbursts in their representation. - Works creatively on a large or small scale (e.g. murals and simple collages).
Evidence and progression notes			

Area of Learning	Creative Development
Focus	Creating Music and Dance

	Development matters	**Dates achieved**	**Examples**
Birth – 11 months	• Respond to a range of familiar sounds, for example, turning to a sound source such as a voice.		• 'Stills' to the sound of music. • Responds to familiar sounds (e.g. a voice).

Evidence and progression notes

	Development matters	**Dates achieved**	**Examples**
8 – 20 months	• Move their whole bodies to sounds they enjoy, such as music or a regular beat.		• Enjoys a one-two rocking rhythm. • Moves arms and legs vigorously to lively music.

Evidence and progression notes

	Development matters	**Dates achieved**	**Examples**
16 – 26 months	• Begin to move to music, listen to or join in rhymes or songs.		• Explores objects by banging. • Makes noises to music. • Rattles a shaker when music is played. • Listens to and sometimes join in rhymes and familiar songs.

Evidence and progression notes

© QEd Publications

Area of Learning	Creative Development
Focus	Creating Music and Dance

	Development matters	**Dates achieved**	**Examples**
22 – 36 months	• Join in singing favourite songs. • Create sounds by banging, shaking, tapping or blowing. • Show an interest in the way musical instruments sound.		• Joins in with some words and actions when favourite songs are sung. • 'Dances' to music (not yet to a beat). • Creates sounds by shaking, banging, tapping things. • Shows interest musical instruments (e.g. pats drum or tambourine).
Evidence and progression notes			

	Development matters	**Dates achieved**	**Examples**
30 – 50 months	• Enjoy joining in with dancing and ring games. • Sing a few familiar songs. • Sing to themselves and make up simple songs. • Tap out simple repeated rhythms and make some up. • Explore and learn how sounds can be changed. • Imitate and create movement in response to music.		• Joins in with dancing and singing games. • Sings a few familiar songs, sometimes making up songs. • Taps out a simple beat with a percussion instrument. • Recognises and explores how sounds can be changed (e.g. playing loudly or softly). • Makes up new ways of moving and dancing to music.
Evidence and progression notes			

Area of Learning	Creative Development
Focus	Creating Music and Dance

	Development matters	Dates achieved	Examples
40 – 60 months	• Begin to build a repertoire of songs and dances. • Explore the different sounds of instruments. • Begin to move rhythmically. • **Recognise and explore how sounds can be changed, sing simple songs from memory, recognise repeated sounds and sound patterns and match movements to music.**		• Can remember a range of dances and songs. • Explores the different sounds instruments make. • Marches or dances to a simple beat. • Dances confidently and freely. • Explores how sounds can be changed (e.g. plays loudly/softly or quickly/slowly in imitation). • Sings and carries out actions at the same time (e.g. joining in 'Wheels on the bus' with words and actions). • Continues a repeated sound pattern (e.g. continues a one-two rhythm when copying an adult).
	Evidence and progression notes		

Area of Learning	Creative Development
Focus	Developing Imagination and Imaginative Play

	Development matters	Dates achieved	Examples
Birth – 11 months	• Smile with pleasure at recognisable playthings.		• Enjoys familiar toys. • Cuddles a teddy or a doll. • Enjoys peek-a-boo games.

Evidence and progression notes

	Development matters	Dates achieved	Examples
8 – 20 months	• Enjoy making noises or movements spontaneously.		• Copies facial expressions (e.g. looks serious when adult does). • Imitates hand clapping • Rolls a car along making noises.

Evidence and progression notes

© QEd Publications

Area of Learning	Creative Development
Focus	Developing Imagination and Imaginative Play

	Development matters	**Dates achieved**	**Examples**
16 – 26 months	• Pretend that one object represents another, especially when objects have characteristics in common.		• Pretends one thing is something else (e.g. 'This box is teddy's bed'). • Pretends to be asleep. • Puts doll into bed or buggy. • Plays on own in home corner.

Evidence and progression notes

	Development matters	**Dates achieved**	**Examples**
22 – 36 months	• Begin to make-believe by pretending.		• Pretends one thing is something else, even if dissimilar (e.g. 'This brush is my horse'). • Acts out pretend scenarios (e.g. have a tea party with the teddies). • Uses different tones of voice in imaginary play. • Enjoys dressing up.

Evidence and progression notes

Area of Learning	Creative Development
Focus	Developing Imagination and Imaginative Play

	Development matters	Dates achieved	Examples
30 – 50 months	• Notice what adults do, imitating what is observed and then doing it spontaneously when the adult is not there. • Use available resources to create props to support role-play. • Develop a repertoire of actions by putting a sequence of movements together. • Engage in imaginative play and role-play based on own first-hand experiences.		• Copies adults doing something in their play. • Finds own props to support their role-play. • Pretends to be someone else. • Enjoys role-play (e.g. in a themed area). • Engages in imaginative play, based on actual experiences.

Evidence and progression notes

	Development matters	Dates achieved	Examples
40 – 60 months	• Introduce a storyline or narrative into their play. • Play alongside other children who are engaged in the same theme. • Play cooperatively as part of a group to act out a narrative. • **Use their imagination in art and design, music, dance, imaginative and role-play and stories.**		• Introduces a storyline into their play (e.g. tells you they are going on holiday). • Plays with puppets with another child. • Plays alongside children engaged in the same theme. • Plays cooperatively in a group to act out a narrative or imaginative game.

Evidence and progression notes

© QEd Publications

General Observation and Planning Form

Activity	Comments	Member of staff/ parent/carer	Date

Final Summative Assessment Comments

Personal, Social and Emotional Development

Communication, Language and Literacy

Problem Solving, Reasoning and Numeracy

Knowledge and Understanding of the World

Physical Development

Creative Development

Parent/Carer Comments	**Key Person Comments**

This should be completed and given to parents/carers prior to children starting school

Assessment scales

Area of Learning	Personal, Social and Emotional Development
Focus	Dispositions and Attitudes

	Date achieved
1. Shows an interest in classroom activities through observation or participation.	
2. Dresses, undresses and manages own personal hygiene with adult support.	
3. Displays high levels of involvement in self-chosen activities.	
4. Dresses and undresses independently and manages own personal hygiene.	
5. Selects and uses activities and resources independently.	
6. Continues to be interested, motivated and excited to learn.	
7. Is confident to try new activities, initiate ideas and speak in a familiar group.	
8. Maintains attention and concentrates.	
9. Sustains involvement and perseveres, particularly when trying to solve a problem or reach a satisfactory conclusion.	

Area of Learning	Personal, Social and Emotional Development
Focus	Social Development

	Date achieved
1. Plays alongside others.	
2. Builds relationships through gesture and talk.	
3. Takes turns and shares with adult support.	
4. Works as part of a group or class taking turns and sharing fairly.	
5. Forms good relationships with adults and peers.	
6. Understands that there need to be agreed values and codes of behaviour for groups of people, including adults and children, to work together harmoniously.	
7. Understands that people have different needs, views, cultures and beliefs that need to be treated with respect.	
8. Understands that (s)he can expect others to treat her or his needs, views, cultures and beliefs with respect.	
9. Takes into account the ideas of others.	

The Assessment scales are taken from **The Early Years Foundation Stage** Statutory Framework

Assessment scales

Area of Learning	Personal, Social and Emotional Development
Focus	Emotional Development

	Date achieved
1. Separates from main carer with support.	
2. Communicates freely about home and community.	
3. Expresses needs and feelings in appropriate ways.	
4. Responds to significant experiences, showing a range of feelings when appropriate.	
5. Has a developing awareness of own needs, views and feelings and is sensitive to the needs, views and feelings of others.	
6. Has a developing respect for own culture and beliefs and those of other people.	
7. Considers the consequences of words and actions for self and others.	
8. Understands what is right, what is wrong and why.	
9. Displays a strong and positive sense of self-identity and is able to express a range of emotions fluently and appropriately.	

Assessment scales

Area of Learning	Communication, Language and Literacy
Focus	Language for Communication and Thinking

	Date achieved
1. Listens and responds.	
2. Initiates communication with others, displaying greater confidence in more informal contexts.	
3. Talks activities through, reflecting on and modifying actions.	
4. Listens with enjoyment to stories, songs, rhymes and poems, sustains attentive listening and responds with relevant comments, questions or actions.	
5. Uses language to imagine and recreate roles and experiences.	
6. Interacts with others in a variety of contexts, negotiating plans and activities and taking turns in conversation.	
7. Uses talk to organise, sequence and clarify thinking, ideas, feelings and events, exploring the meanings and sounds of new words.	
8. Speaks clearly with confidence and control, showing awareness of the listener.	
9. Talks and listens confidently and with control, consistently showing awareness of the listener by including relevant detail. Uses language to work out and clarify ideas, showing control of a range of appropriate vocabulary.	

The Assessment scales are taken from **The Early Years Foundation Stage** Statutory Framework

Assessment scales

Area of Learning	Communication, Language and Literacy
Focus	Linking Sounds and Letters

	Date achieved
1. Joins in with rhyming and rhythmic activities.	
2. Shows an awareness of rhyme and alliteration.	
3. Links some sounds to letters.	
4. Links sounds to letters, naming and sounding letters of the alphabet.	
5. Hears and says sounds in words.	
6. Blends sounds in words.	
7. Uses phonic knowledge to read simple regular words.	
8. Attempts to read more complex words, using phonic knowledge.	
9. Uses knowledge of letters, sounds and words when reading and writing independently.	

Area of Learning	Communication, Language and Literacy
Focus	Reading

	Date achieved
1. Is developing an interest in books.	
2. Knows that print conveys meaning.	
3. Recognises a few familiar words.	
4. Knows that, in English, print is read from left to right and top to bottom.	
5. Shows an understanding of the elements of stories, such as main character, sequence of events and openings.	
6. Reads a range of familiar and common words and simple sentences independently.	
7. Retells narratives in the correct sequence, drawing on language patterns of stories.	
8. Shows an understanding of how information can be found in non-fiction texts to answer questions about where, who, why and how.	
9. Reads books of own choice with some fluency and accuracy.	

The Assessment scales are taken from **The Early Years Foundation Stage** Statutory Framework

Assessment scales

Area of Learning	Communication, Language and Literacy
Focus	Writing

	Date achieved
1. Experiments with mark-making, sometimes ascribing meaning to the marks.	
2. Uses some clearly identifiable letters to communicate meaning.	
3. Represents some sounds correctly in writing.	
4. Writes own name and other words from memory.	
5. Holds a pencil and uses it effectively to form recognisable letters, most of which are correctly formed.	
6. Attempts writing for a variety of purposes, using features of different forms.	
7. Uses phonic knowledge to write simple regular words and make phonetically plausible attempts at more complex words.	
8. Begins to form captions and simple sentences, sometimes using punctuation.	
9. Communicates meaning through phrases and simple sentences with some consistency in punctuating sentences.	

Assessment scales

Area of Learning	Problem Solving, Reasoning and Numeracy
Focus	Numbers as Labels and for Counting

	Date achieved
1. Says some number names in familiar contexts, such as nursery rhymes.	
2. Counts reliably up to three everyday objects.	
3. Counts reliably up to six everyday objects.	
4. Says number names in order.	
5. Recognises numerals 1 to 9.	
6. Counts reliably up to ten everyday objects.	
7. Orders numbers, up to ten.	
8. Uses developing mathematical ideas and methods to solve practical problems.	
9. Recognises, counts, orders, writes and uses numbers up to 20.	

The Assessment scales are taken from **The Early Years Foundation Stage** Statutory Framework

Assessment scales

Area of Learning	Problem Solving, Reasoning and Numeracy
Focus	Calculating

	Date achieved
1. Responds to the vocabulary involved in addition and subtraction in rhymes and games.	
2. Recognises differences in quantity when comparing sets of objects.	
3. Finds one more or less from a group of up to five objects.	
4. Relates addition to combining two groups.	
5. Relates subtraction to taking away.	
6. In practical activities and discussion, begins to use the vocabulary involved in adding and subtracting.	
7. Finds one more or one less than a number from one to ten.	
8. Uses developing mathematical ideas and methods to solve practical problems.	
9. Uses a range of strategies for addition and subtraction, including some mental recall of number bonds.	

Area of Learning	Problem Solving, Reasoning and Numeracy
Focus	Shape, Space and Measures

	Date achieved
1. Experiments with a range of objects and materials showing some mathematical awareness.	
2. Sorts or matches objects and talks about sorting.	
3. Describes shapes in simple models, pictures and patterns.	
4. Talks about, recognises and recreates simple patterns.	
5. Uses everyday words to describe position.	
6. Uses language such as 'circle' or 'bigger' to describe the shape and size of solids and flat shapes.	
7. Uses language such as 'greater', 'smaller', 'heavier' or 'lighter' to compare quantities.	
8. Uses developing mathematical ideas and methods to solve practical problems.	
9. Uses mathematical language to describe solid (3D) objects and flat (2D) shapes.	

The Assessment scales are taken from **The Early Years Foundation Stage** Statutory Framework

Assessment scales

Area of Learning	Knowledge and Understanding of the World

	Date achieved
1. Shows curiosity and interest by exploring surroundings.	
2. Observes, selects and manipulates objects and materials. Identifies simple features and significant personal events.	
3. Identifies obvious similarities and differences when exploring and observing. Constructs in a purposeful way, using simple tools and techniques.	
4. Investigates places, objects, materials and living things by using all the senses as appropriate. Identifies some features and talks about those features (s)he likes and dislikes.	
5. Asks questions about why things happen and how things work. Looks closely at similarities, differences, patterns and change.	
6. Finds out about past and present events in own life, and in those of family members and other people (s)he knows. Begins to know about own culture and beliefs and those of other people.	
7. Finds out about and identifies the uses of everyday technology and uses information and communication technology and programmable toys to support her/his learning.	
8. Builds and constructs with a wide range of objects, selecting appropriate resources, tools and techniques and adapting her/his work where necessary.	
9. Communicates simple planning for investigations and constructions and makes simple records and evaluations of her/his work. Identifies and names key features and properties, sometimes linking different experiences, observations and events. Begins to explore what it means to belong to a variety of groups and communities.	

The Assessment scales are taken from **The Early Years Foundation Stage** Statutory Framework

Assessment scales

Area of Learning	Physical Development

	Date achieved
1. Moves spontaneously, showing some control and coordination.	
2. Moves with confidence in a variety of ways, showing some awareness of space.	
3. Usually shows appropriate control in large- and small-scale movements.	
4. Moves with confidence, imagination and safety. Travels around, under, over and through balancing and climbing equipment. Shows awareness of space, of self and others.	
5. Demonstrates fine motor control and coordination.	
6. Uses small and large equipment, showing a range of basic skills.	
7. Handles tools, objects, construction and malleable materials safely and with basic control.	
8. Recognises the importance of keeping healthy and those things which contribute to this. Recognises the changes that happen to her/his body when s/he is active.	
9. Repeats, links and adapts simple movements, sometimes commenting on her/his work. Demonstrates coordination and control in large and small movements, and in using a range of tools and equipment.	

The Assessment scales are taken from **The Early Years Foundation Stage** Statutory Framework

Assessment scales

Area of Learning	Creative Development

	Date achieved
1. Explores different media and responds to a variety of sensory experiences. Engages in representational play.	
2. Creates simple representations of events, people and objects and engages in music making.	
3. Tries to capture experiences, using a variety of different media.	
4. Sings simple songs from memory.	
5. Explores colour, texture, shape, form and space in two or three dimensions.	
6. Recognises and explores how sounds can be changed. Recognises repeated sounds and sound patterns and matches movements to music.	
7. Uses imagination in art and design, music, dance, imaginative and role-play and stories. Responds in a variety of ways to what (s)he sees, hears, smells, touches and feels.	
8. Expresses and communicates ideas, thoughts and feelings using a range of materials, suitable tools, imaginative and role-play, movement, designing and making, and a variety of songs and musical instruments.	
9. Expresses feelings and preferences in response to artwork, drama and music and makes some comparisons and links between different pieces. Responds to own work and that of others when exploring and communicating ideas, feelings, and preferences through art, music, dance, role-play and imaginative play.	

The Assessment scales are taken from **The Early Years Foundation Stage** Statutory Framework